THE WORST-CASE SCENARIO
ALMANAC
POLITICS

D0036699

The
WORST-CASE SCENARIO
ALMANAC
POLITICS

**By David Borgenicht
& Turk Regan**

Illustrations by Brenda Brown

WITHDRAWN

CHRONICLE BOOKS

SAN FRANCISCO

Copyright © 2008 by Quirk Productions, Inc.

All rights reserved. No part of this book may be reproduced in any form without written permission from the publisher.

Worst-Case Scenario® and The Worst-Case Scenario Survival Handbook™ are trademarks of Quirk Productions, Inc.

Library of Congress Cataloging-in-Publication Data available.
ISBN: 978-0-8118-6321-6

Manufactured in Canada
Typeset in Adobe Caslon, Bundesbahn Pi, Futura, and Zapf Dingbats
Designed by Karen Onorato
Illustrations by Brenda Brown
Graphs illustrated by Bob O'Mara

Visit www.worstcasescenarios.com

10 9 8 7 6 5 4 3 2 1

Chronicle Books LLC
680 Second Street
San Francisco, California 94107
www.chroniclebooks.com

WARNING

When a life is imperiled or a dire situation is at hand, safe alternatives may not exist. To deal with the worst-case scenarios presented in this book, we highly recommend—insist, actually—that the best course of action is to consult a professionally trained expert. But because highly trained professionals may not always be available when the safety or sanity of individuals is at risk, we have asked experts on various subjects to describe the techniques they might employ in these emergency situations. THE PUBLISHER, AUTHORS, AND EXPERTS DISCLAIM ANY LIABILITY from any injury that may result from the use, proper or improper, of the information contained in this book. All the answers in this book come from experts in the situation at hand, but we do not guarantee that the information contained herein is complete, safe, or accurate, nor should it be considered a substitute for your good judgment or common sense. And finally, nothing in this book should be construed or interpreted to infringe on the rights of other persons or to violate criminal statutes; we urge you to obey all laws and respect all rights, including property rights, of others, even politicians.

—The Authors

CONTENTS

Politics is still the greatest
and most honorable adventure.
—John Buchan, Lord Tweedsmuir,
Pilgrim's Way, 1940

★ ★ ★ ★ ★

An honest politician is one who when
he's bought stays bought.
—Simon Cameron, U.S. financier and politician
(1799–1889)

★ ★ ★ ★ ★

Under every stone lurks a politician.
—Aristophanes, 410 BC

INTRODUCTION

There is nothing in the world more unpredictable than politics.

There's no human undertaking that we speak about regularly in such contradictory terms. Some people see politics as hopeful, as essential to achieving humanity's dreams and potential. Others see it as a necessary evil, a scam, or a conspiracy of the elite. And they're all correct.

But no matter how you see it, surviving in the world of politics is not easy. At least, it's not "easy" compared to surviving shark attacks or tsunamis, or falling on the subway tracks. In the *Worst-Case Scenario* series of handbooks and almanacs, we showed you how to survive those disasters. But in politics, the landscape, the dangers, the ways to survive are constantly changing. Politics is about people, and politics is about power, and you just can't count on being safe with either one.

Your motives might be good (or not), but in politics, you might think you've made it safely out of a bad situation, you can think you're on top, or at least that you've gained a foothold, but something always will come up to try to knock you off your pedestal. Chairman Mao aptly called it "war without bloodshed," though Winston Churchill pointed out that in war you can be killed only once, "but in politics, many times."

And that's where this book comes in. In an effort to provide help to those who have committed themselves to a career in the political arena, we've compiled an incredibly useful and rather effective almanac. The lessons of the past are combined with step-by-step instructions on surviving a variety of crises of today, along with charts, diagrams, and profiles of the infamous. With this book you can feel safer when you throw your hat into the ring—and have detailed instructions on how to avoid having to eat it later.

First you have to get elected ("How to Pretend You Care") and deal with the media ("How to Work a Hostile Room"), then deal with scandals ("How to Open an Offshore Bank Account") and plans gone awry ("How to Smuggle Yourself Out of the Country"). It's all here. Presidents, world leaders, and even Machiavelli would have a lot to learn from *The Worst-Case Scenario Almanac: Politics*.

You just never know what will happen in politics, so be ready. And ask not what you can do to your country, but what Worst-Case can do for you.

—The Authors

SEIZING POWER

YOUTHFUL INDISCRETIONS

Who	Later in Life	Indiscretion
Constantine V	Emperor of the Holy Roman Empire (741–775)	Defecated in his baptismal font
Benito Mussolini	Fascist ruler of Italy (1922–45)	Banned from church as a child for throwing rocks at the congregation; expelled from grade school for stabbing a fellow student and hurling his ink pot at a teacher
Ivan IV	Czar of Russia (1544–84)	Threw cats and dogs from the high windows of his palace as a child; as a teenager joined a violent street gang known for attacking the elderly
Golda Meir	Prime Minister of Israel (1969–74)	Ran away at the age of 14 and lived 1,000 miles away for over a year before returning home
Viktor Yanukovych	President of Ukraine (2002–05, 2006–07)	Convicted as a teenager on separate occasions for assault and robbery
Joschka Fischer	Vice-Chancellor of Germany (1998–2005)	Led the anarchist youth group Revolutionary Combat, which often attacked policemen, seriously injuring several officers
Trent Lott	U.S. Senate Majority Leader (1996–2001)	Served as a male cheerleader while attending the University of Mississippi

YOUNG LBJ STEALS STUDENT ELECTIONS, DISCOVERS LIFE'S CALLING

Lyndon B. Johnson was perhaps the least popular student during his freshman year at Southwest Texas State Teachers' College. But through campus politics and pioneering experiments in election fraud, the gawky, boasting, and brown-nosing Johnson became one of the school's most prominent students. Johnson was rejected when he tried to join the college's most popular fraternity, the White Stars. He was also initially rejected from the secret society that opposed them, the Black Stars, until Johnson hatched a plan that would allow the Black Stars to take over the White Stars–dominated student government. He dug up embarrassing information to intimidate White Stars candidates into withdrawing. He also masterminded plans to keep rival candidates off the ballot, allow his cronies to vote multiple times, and dispose of ballots cast by the opposition. He even advocated the practice of strategic dating—having his fellow Black Stars romance girls to influence their votes, then breaking up with them after election day. Johnson's leadership and chicanery led the Black Stars to victory. After graduating, Johnson applied the lessons he had learned at college to national politics. During his 1948 run for a United States Senate seat in Texas, Johnson supposedly had election officials in friendly counties withhold results until he knew how many votes he needed to win. Just when it looked like he had lost by a little over 100 votes, a "missing" ballot box from Duval County was discovered containing 203 ballots, 202 of which were marked for Johnson, and the voters had mysteriously cast their ballots in exact alphabetical order.

Political Lesson: Start learning early and apply what works again and again.

Playground Politics
Applying Childhood Lessons to Political Situations

Political Problem	Childhood Equivalent	Childhood Solution	Political Solution
Powerful rival threatens to humiliate you	**Bully threatens to beat you up**	**Avert bully's attention to get him to beat up some kid you both don't like**	**Cut deal with rival to get him to humiliate one of your mutual enemies**
Caught taking donation from dubious source	**Caught with hand in cookie jar**	**Blame inadequacy of previous meal served by your parents**	**Blame the system for forcing politicians to raise so much money**
No time to read bill coming up for vote	**No time to write school book report**	**Bribe school nerd to do it for you**	**Order staffer to read bill and brief you on key points**
Low standing in public opinion polls	**Unpopular at school**	**Copy what the popular kids are doing**	**Jump on the bandwagon of a popular political cause**
Interest group refuses to endorse you	**Would-be prom date snubs you**	**Circulate rumors that would-be date has social disease**	**Circulate rumors that group leadership faces impending scandal**
Taunted by rivals for embarrassing incident	**Teased by classmates over embarrassing incident**	**Beat up the weakest of them**	**Publicly humiliate your weakest rival**

HOW TO DEAL WITH A FAMILY LIABILITY

EMBARRASSING PARENT

⭐ Distinguish yourself in virtues that contradict your parent's main vices.
Highlight how much time and money you dedicate to organizations that combat drunk drivers and alcoholism, if one or both of your parents is a well-known lush.

⭐ Transform your parent's vices into a positive campaign issue.
Speak out against gambling, drugs, stealing, lying, fraud, or lechery, saying you know firsthand about the damage it can do. Point out your ability to overcome the adversity caused by the problem.

⭐ Accentuate the positive.
Talk of your warm childhood memories and all the gratitude you feel for the positive things that your parent did for you and the positive traits you inherited.

⭐ Make amends.
Offer financial compensation to people victimized by your parent's bad behavior. If the financial reward would be too onerous or legally treacherous, volunteer your time to them.

Distinguish yourself from your family's faults and vices.

SLEAZY SIBLING

★ Do not allow your sibling to work for your campaign.
Refuse all offers of help. Reject attempts by your ne'er-do-well sibling to obtain a job or to attach him- or herself in any other way to your political career.

★ Ban your sibling.
Forbid your sibling from attending any of your business, social, and campaign appearances.

★ Keep your distance.
A recent photo of you with your sibling could be used by your opponents. At a family gathering or other event you and your sleazy sibling both attend, maintain a distance of at least ten yards to prevent anyone from snapping a picture of you together.

★ Highlight your relationships with acceptable family members.
Arrange for numerous pictures to be taken of you with your arm around your virtuous siblings and other well-behaved relatives. These photos will visually emphasize your commitment to family, while further distancing you from your sleazy sibling.

★ Refuse to discuss your sleazy sibling in public.
If reporters or constituents ask you about the sins and vices of your sibling, answer by saying you would prefer not to discuss private family matters.

Plant stories about the scandalous siblings of successful politicians.
Have aides remind reporters of far sleazier siblings of politicians. Point out that these politicians did not let their siblings keep them from doing a good job in office.

Cheating Spouse

 Throw good love after bad.
Talk about how love, loyalty, and your commitment to the institution of marriage have kept you together, despite your spouse's shortcomings and vices.

 Be forgiving, but wary.
Do not to appear too accepting of your spouse's shortcomings in order to avoid looking gullible or like an easy victim.

 Focus on the big picture.
Refuse to review the lurid details of your marriage with reporters and instead discuss in general terms the need for forgiveness and growth in any relationship.

Problem Child

 Identify with others.
Be active in organizations dedicated to children and parents going through the same problems that your family is experiencing.

★ Emphasize how you and your spouse embrace the child's problems.

Have aides place stories in the media about how you have always gone to great lengths to give the child everything he or she needs and to guide the child onto the right path in life.

★ Keep your child out of sight.

Send your problem child to camps or schools in remote places or sign him or her up for rehabilitation clinics for extended stays during key periods in your campaign.

Political Brief

In 1927, Charles D.B. King won reelection as president of Liberia by a margin of more than 234,000 votes. At the time, Liberia had fewer than 15,000 registered voters. King was later ousted as head of Liberia, which had been founded by freed American slaves in 1820, when a 1930 League of Nations report revealed King was engaged in slave trading, selling his poor constituents to forced labor camps run by international business interests that contributed heavily to his campaign.

MARY QUEEN OF SCOTS WEDS A JACK OF KNAVES

Handsome Englishman Lord Darnley won the favor of young widow Mary I, Queen of Scots, upon his arrival to the Scottish court in 1565. A descendant of deceased British King Henry VII, Darnley boasted a royal lineage that would not only help Mary solidify her hold on the Scottish throne, but also all but guarantee their off-spring would become the next British and Scottish monarch. Declaring Darnley "the best proportioned long man that I have ever seen," Mary married him in 1565. But the 19-year-old Darnley proved himself arrogant, cruel, immature, and surprisingly stupid. He squandered most of Mary's money, much of it on women's cloth-ing for himself. An alcoholic, Darnley would go out in public in drag and berate his wife and her supporters. Despite his growing unpop-ularity, Darnley insisted Mary designate him as co-ruler of Scotland. When she refused, he organized a gang to murder Mary's close advisor David Riccio in front of the appalled Queen. Darnley then beat Mary and locked her in her bedroom. He hoped the shock of the murder, physical abuse, and incarceration would cause the pregnant Queen to miscarry—thus eliminating Darnley's future rival to the Scottish and English thrones. After escaping, Mary lured the gullible Darnley to a "reconciliation" at an Edinburgh cot-tage, which blew up in the middle of the night shortly after Mary crept away from her sleeping husband. Darnley was found dead in the rubble in the morning. Though welcomed by nearly everyone in Scotland, Darnley's murder allowed Mary's powerful rival Queen Elizabeth of England to arrest Mary the following year on the legal pretense that Darnley was technically an English subject.

Political Lesson: Appearances count, but don't be fooled by a pretty face.

BAD SIBLINGS

Politician	Position	Infamous Sibling(s)	Infamous Act(s)
Hillary Clinton	U.S. First Lady (1993–2001); U.S. Senator (2003–)	Tony and Hugh Rodham	Partnered with a Russian mafia figure on a $118 million hazelnut export scheme; both brothers were involved in a drunken brawl with the husband of a woman Tony picked up in a bar
Publius Clodius	Roman Patrician & Tribune (1st Century BC)	Clodia Metelli	"The Medea of the Palatine" was a degenerate gambler, alcoholic, and nymphomaniac who triggered numerous scandals, including a lurid murder trial that shamed her into hiding for the rest of her life
John II	Ruler of Byzantine Empire (1118–43)	Anna Comnena	Conspired with her mother in failed attempt to overthrow her brother and replace him on the throne with her husband
King Sansang	Ruler of Northern Korea (AD 196–227)	Balgi	Refused to accept his younger brother as king; gathered an army to invade the capital before being defeated and forced to commit suicide
Ptolemy XIV	Co-Ruler of Egypt (47–44 BC)	Cleopatra VII	Poisoned her younger brother/husband and co-ruler so she could put her son Caesarion in his place
Giovanni Borgia	Duke of Palestrina (1501–48)	Cesare Borgia	Carried on an affair with his younger brother Jofre's wife; murdered older brother Giovanni when he found out he was having an affair with her as well

JIMMY CARTER'S BOORISH BROTHER HELPS UNDERMINE HIS PRESIDENCY

Runaway inflation, the humiliating Iran hostage crisis, and a weak economy all contributed to incumbent Jimmy Carter's landslide loss in the 1980 U.S. presidential election, but Carter's little brother did more than his share to push Jimmy to the worst defeat ever suffered by a sitting U.S. president. Billy Carter was a self-described "real Southern boy" with "a red neck, white socks, and Blue Ribbon beer." When his clean-cut brother Jimmy, the governor of Georgia, became the surprise Democratic presidential nominee, the media descended on Carter's tiny hometown of Plains, Georgia, to find out more about the relatively obscure politician. Billy regaled the press corps with his excessive beer drinking, belches, bawdy jokes, embarrassing family stories, and outrageous acts. While waiting for a plane with a group of foreign dignitaries and reporters, he pulled down his fly in front of everyone and urinated on the tarmac. In 1980, while his brother Jimmy was running for reelection, newspaper stories emerged revealing that Billy had taken over $200,000 in "loans" to lobby the president on behalf of Libya. Jimmy Carter, who built his presidency around promises of honesty and integrity, saw his approval ratings plummet.

Political Lesson: Be your brother's keeper, at least until the election is over.

Political Brief

President Lyndon Johnson had the Secret Service keep his brother, Sam Johnson, under house arrest at the White House in the months leading up to the 1964 election. The president was trying to curtail his little brother's habit of getting drunk in Washington, D.C., bars, where reporters would ply him with free drinks and get him to reveal embarrassing information about the president.

MARK THATCHER
Political Problem Child

WORST DEEDS: Embarrassing his mother with a series of scandals and mishaps throughout her tenure as prime minister of England from 1979 to 1990 ★ Being arrested for financing a failed coup d'etat in the African nation of Equatorial Guinea ★ Getting caught running a loan shark operation in South Africa ★ Being deported from Monaco for racketeering ★ Getting lost for six days when he strayed 30 miles off course during a sports car rally in the Sahara Desert ★ Making millions of dollars in commissions by winning lucrative contracts for his clients from the British government while his mother was prime minister ★ Disparaging American billionaire and philanthropist Walter Annenberg during a dinner party in Annenberg's home for serving claret in the wrong-shaped glasses

BORN: August 15, 1953 in London, England

FAMILY: Twin Sister: Carol, a journalist ★ Father: Sir Denis Thatcher (1915–2003), a baron and successful businessman ★ Mother: Margaret Thatcher (1925–), British prime minister (1979–1990)

NICKNAMES: "Thickie Mork," "Scratcher," "The Mark Problem"

EDUCATION: Attended Harrow, a prestigious private school in West London

FIRST JOB: Dismissed from Touche Ross, a London accounting firm, after he failed three times to pass the official exam to gain a professional accounting license

QUOTE: "Leave the country." —Margaret Thatcher's press secretary Bernard Ingham, after Mark asked him what he could do to help his mother win reelection in 1987

MEHMET III LEAVES NO DOUBT OF MALE RELATIVE UPON BECOMING SULTAN

Murdering all your close male relatives had become part of the inauguration process for new Ottoman sultans during the 15th century—a practice aimed to head off battles of succession and civil wars amongst the sons and nephews of a dying sultan. But Sultan Mehmet III, who took over as head of the Ottoman Empire in 1595, took to the tradition with unusual zeal, killing not just his two dozen brothers and nephews, but also murdering more than twenty of his sisters to ensure they would not produce any more male offspring to challenge his position. Mehmet III's reign over the Ottoman Empire was, for the most part, administered by his mother; once Mehmet had murdered his way to the top, he showed little interest in governance. When compelled to take the field in a war against Austria's Hapsburg Empire, the sultan had to be restrained by his lieutenants from fleeing the battlefield. The following year, Mehmet III was excused from further military duty when his doctors declared that he had become too fat from his royal life of indolence and gluttony to serve as an effective general.

Political Lesson: The ties that bind can also be used to strangle.

Political Brief

Caesar Augustus, the first emperor of Rome, became so appalled by the infidelities and treacheries of his daughter and only child, Julia, that he exiled her to live alone on Pandateria, a desolate island in the Mediterranean Sea only a half-mile in width.

PROBLEM CHILDREN

Politician	Position	Child	Problem	Delinquency Rating
Kim Jong-il	Leader of North Korea (1994–)	Kim Jong-nam	Made numerous secret trips to Japan to visit prostitutes before being caught in Tokyo traveling under an assumed name and claiming he was there to visit Disneyland	★★
Joan Mont	Head of England's East Sussex County Council (1989–1991)	Fiona "The Cat" Mont	Escaped twice from police after being arrested for corporate fraud, becoming a media sensation and Britain's "Most Wanted Woman" during a three-year fugitive run across Europe with her drug smuggler boyfriend Graham "The Baron" Hesketh	★★★
Suharto	President of Indonesia (1967–98)	Tommy Suharto	Hired a hitman to kill a judge who had found him guilty of corruption	★★★★
Saddam Hussein	President of Iraq (1979–2003)	Uday	Murdered his father's old friend and personal assistant Kamal Hana Gegeo at a state party with an electric carving knife	★★★★
Birendra Bir Bikram Shah Dev	King of Nepal (1972–2001)	Prince Dipendra	Got drunk, grabbed an M16 rifle, and shot to death his father, mother, and siblings, then himself	★★★★★

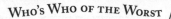

MESSALINA

Nymphomaniac and Roman Empress

Worst Deeds: Marrying Claudius Caesar Augustus at the behest of Emperor Caligula, then becoming empress when Claudius succeeded Caligula as head of the Roman Empire in AD 41 ★ Committing bigamy while Claudius was out of town on official business by marrying the Roman Senator Silius at a public wedding ceremony and encouraging him to murder Claudius upon the emperor's return to Rome ★ Staging an all-night sex contest between the legendary Roman prostitute Scylla and herself to determine who could fornicate with more men in one night; an exhausted Scylla conceded defeat at dawn, with the Empress Messalina still eager to continue ★ Using her vast wealth and power to have her rivals, or anyone who refused to sleep with her, murdered or exiled ★ Gaining the honor of sitting in the front row with the Vestal Virgins at public events

Born: AD 17 or 20

Died: AD 48

Nickname: "The Wolf Girl"

Education: Unknown, though given her family's status, likely as well-educated as any woman in Rome

First job: Wealthy even before she became empress, Messalina did not need to work, but still moonlighted at a Roman brothel in a blonde wig using her "Wolf Girl" alias while her husband Claudius slept back in the royal palace

Quote: "Your life is finished. All that remains is to make a decent end." —Messalina's mother, Lepida, urging Messalina to commit suicide after her husband sent soldiers to execute her following the failed attempt to overthrow him. She could not bear to kill herself, and was killed by Claudius's soldiers.

QUARREL WITH WIFE TURNS POPULAR GOVERNOR INTO LYNCH MOB TARGET

Sam Houston transformed from the most promising young politician in the United States to a hunted fugitive fleeing the country, all due to an argument with his wife. In the spring of 1829, Houston was serving his first term as governor of his native Tennessee. The personable Houston was viewed as a lock for reelection as governor in the autumn and as the leading contender to eventually succeed his mentor Andrew Jackson as U.S. president. Houston had bolstered his political status by marrying into a wealthy and powerful Nashville dynasty. But his arranged marriage to 18-year-old Eliza Allen never developed into romance. One afternoon, Houston and Eliza fell into a heated argument when she reportedly told Houston she loved another. Word leaked out that Houston responded by accusing Eliza of infidelity. Questioning the virtue of an aristocratic woman was still a serious offense in the early 19th-century American South. Mobs gathered in the streets outside the governor's mansion and burned Houston in effigy. Fearing he would be lynched by his constituents, Houston fled Nashville. He was forced to resign as governor and promised never to return to Tennessee.
Political Lesson: Trouble at home leads to trouble in office.

Skeletons in the Closet

Politician	Skeleton in Closet
Kurt Waldheim President of Austria (1986–92); Secretary General of the United Nations (1972–82)	Served as a Nazi army officer during World War II, stationed at one point a few miles from a concentration camp
Philomena Bijlhout Dutch Minister for Emancipation and Family Affairs (2002)	Was forced to resign as a Dutch cabinet member when an old photo revealed she had been part of a Surinam militia infamous for murdering its political opponents
Tenzin Gyatso the 14th Dalai Lama, Head of State in Tibet (1950–59)	Had longtime ties to the CIA, which paid him millions of dollars, including funds to form a guerilla army
Thomas Eagleton Democratic nominee for vice president (1972)	Was confined in a mental hospital on three occasions, twice receiving electro-shock therapy
Allen Yancey Vice President of Liberia (1928–30)	Forced to resign after a League of Nations report identified him as a slave trader
Benito Mussolini Fascist ruler of Italy (1922–45)	Dodged military service as a young man by fleeing to Switzerland

HOW TO WORK A RECEIVING LINE DURING FLU SEASON

⭐ Assume a defensive posture.

Position yourself so that you are standing beside, rather than in front of, a coughing or otherwise potentially contagious voter. Put one arm around the voter's shoulders, then move shoulder-to-shoulder with him. Face the same direction, so his hacking and breathing projects away from you instead of at you.

⭐ Practice intermittent breathing.

If a contagious voter is unavoidably standing directly in front of you, take short, shallow breaths. Turn your nose and mouth to one side to avoid his potentially infectious exhalation, all the while maintaining eye contact with the voter. Then, reload your lungs with long, deep breaths while facing skyward after the person leaves and before the next germ carrier shows up in front of you.

⭐ Do not shake hands.

Avoid shaking hands—an action that can transmit numerous germs—with infectious voters whenever possible. Instead, make a preemptive move to initiate contact by clapping the voter on the back or grabbing his elbow or forearm. Pat a child on the very top of the head.

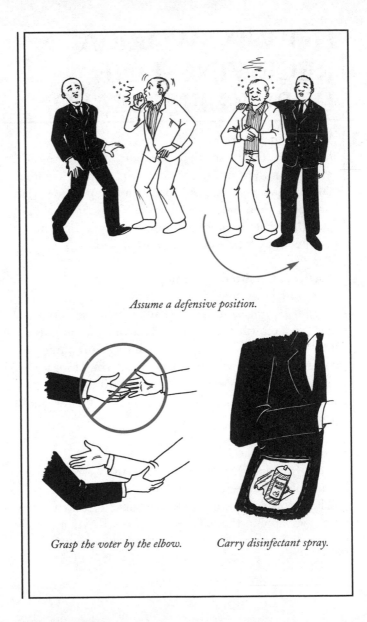

Assume a defensive position.

Grasp the voter by the elbow.

Carry disinfectant spray.

★ Do not touch your face.
Shaking hands transmits millions of germs onto the surfaces of your fingers and palm. Avoid transferring these germs to your nose and mouth—increasing your chance of infection—by resisting any impulse to touch your face until you are properly able to decontaminate yourself.

★ Disinfect clandestinely.
Keep a small bottle of disinfectant spray and a handkerchief in your pocket. Between unavoidable contact with contagious constituents, reach into your pocket and surreptitiously spritz a bit of disinfectant onto your hand, wiping it on the handkerchief placed beside it in the pocket. Withdraw your hand and continue greeting voters.

THE MAN WHO WOULDN'T BE KING

Though he came from a foreign, working-class family with no connection to British royalty, Perkin Warbeck spent his adult life trying to convince people that he was the long-lost King of England. Born around 1474 in Flanders, young Warbeck worked as a servant for a number of minor aristocrats around Europe. He came to the attention of the House of York, the exiled British dynasty looking to reclaim the British throne from King Henry VII of the House of Tudor. Henry VII had seized the throne from the last York King, Richard III, in 1485. Noting Warbeck's physical resemblance to them, the Yorks recruited him to pretend that he actually was their long-deceased kin Richard of Shrewsbury—the son of the former English monarch Edward IV. Shrewsbury had been murdered years before by his uncle Richard III. But if he were still alive, he would be, in the eyes of the Yorks and many others, the legitimate King of England. Henry VII's other enemies in Europe welcomed Warbeck to their courts with the pomp and circumstance befitting a true British monarch. King James IV of Scotland even married Warbeck to his eldest daughter. James, along with several other European monarchs, gave Warbeck money, ships, and soldiers to go to England, ignite a civil war, and claim the throne. After two aborted efforts, Warbeck finally invaded England in 1497. Landing at Cornwall, he proclaimed himself King Richard IV in broken English and was joined by a few hundred tax-protesting peasants. But Warbeck fled at the first sight of English forces and was captured a few days later, hiding in a convent. Just like Richard of Shrewsbury, the person he was impersonating, Warbeck was imprisoned in the Tower of London, and then executed.

Political Lesson: Be careful what you pretend to be, you just might become it.

POSITIONS HELD BY PROMINENT POLITICIANS BEFORE TAKING OFFICE

Who	Power Position	Previous Position
Zhu Yuanzhang	Chinese Emperor (1368–98) and founder of the Ming Dynasty	Cowboy
Mansa Sakura	Emperor of Mali (1285–1300)	Slave
Hideo Higashikokubaru	Governor of Miyazaki in Japan (2007–)	Comedian
Incitatus	Equine Roman Senator (AD 39–41)	Favorite horse of Emperor Caligula
Tom DeLay	Majority Leader of U.S. House of Representatives (2003–05)	Pest exterminator
Conrad Burns	U.S. Senator (1989–2007)	Livestock auctioneer
Yasuo Tanaka	Governor of Nagano, Japan (2000–06)	Sex columnist

Political Brief

Robert Casey, who eventually served as governor of Pennsylvania from 1987–95, had lost two earlier elections when opponents convinced other men named Robert Casey to run against him. The confusion cost him the 1976 election for state treasurer and 1978 nomination for lieutenant governor.

ITALIAN PORN STAR ELECTED TO NATION'S PARLIAMENT

Ilona Staller remains the only person to make the jump from starring in pornographic films to a leading role in national politics. After a decade working as a fashion model in Italy, the Hungarian-born Staller extended her talents into radio in 1973, hosting the popular show *Will You Sleep with Me Tonight?*. Two years later, Staller made her debut in adult cinema under her stage name "Cicciolina" (Cuddles). She went on to perform a wide range of sexual acts in more than three dozen pornographic films, including *Backfield in Motion*, *Bestiality*, and *Pornopoker 2*. In 1987, Staller widened the scope of her career again by running for a seat in the Italian Parliament as a member of the Radical Party. Bored with the usual choices, voters elected Staller, whose campaign slogan was "Down with Nuclear Energy, Up with Sexual Energy." She celebrated her victory with supporters gathered in Rome's Piazza Navona by exposing her breasts. Staller showed up for her first day in Parliament in a sequined green gown accompanied by four young women in lingerie. During her five-year term in Italy's legislative body, she worked as an advocate for nuclear disarmament, human rights, animal rights, antipoverty measures, and world peace. She also continued to act in pornographic films. Staller formed her own political party, Partito dell'Amore ("The Party of Love") and ran for reelection in 1992 with stripper Moanna Pazzi as her running mate. She gained only 1 percent of the vote, as her constituents had grown weary of her combination of amoral personal behavior and moral grandstanding.

Political Lesson: You need more than just one gimmick to sustain your political career.

Résumé Euphemisms

What You Did	What to Call It
Worked for a company with a Web site	Internet pioneer
Ran failed businesses	Experienced entrepreneur
Filed bankruptcy	Fiscal realist
Grew backyard tomatoes	Small farm owner
Had children	Child advocate
Got fired	Friend of the working people
Been arrested	Experienced with law enforcement
Dropped out of college	Learned by experience
Took inconsistent positions on issues	Maverick

Political Brief

Shaka Zulu, King of South Africa's Zulu Tribe from 1818–29, was named after a parasite. When his unmarried mother became pregnant by a Zulu chief, she told people the swelling in her stomach was caused by a parasitic beetle or "shaka" that often infected the digestive systems of area people. After he was born, people called him "Shaka" as an insult, but he and his mother decided to stick with the moniker as an act of defiance.

EDGAR ALLAN POE DIES OF VOTER FRAUD

American fiction writer and poet Edgar Allan Poe was found unconscious on the streets of Baltimore outside Gunner's Hall, a bar and polling station, on October 3, 1849—Election Day. The eminent author was badly beaten, intoxicated, and wearing another man's ill-fitting boots and clothing. Most literary scholars believe that Poe had been a victim of "cooping," a common 19th-century voting fraud scheme in which political gangs kidnapped people off the streets, locked them in a room or "coop," plied them with alcohol, and beat them into submission. The victims were then shuttled from polling station to polling station to cast numerous ballots in the same election. They were often forced to change clothes so they could make additional loops around the polling stations without being recognized as someone who had already voted. Some respected biographers and scholars have offered alternative theories of how Poe came to his sorry state, including mugging, alcohol abuse, and an assault by a jealous lover, but none offers a satisfactory explanation for why Poe was found in an old, ill-fitting set of clothes that were not his own, or why he was so close to a polling station where cooping was commonly practiced. After being found, Poe was moved to a hospital. He drifted in and out of consciousness over the next few days, but never became coherent enough to explain what had happened to him. He died early in the morning on October 7, 1849.

Political Lesson: Corrupt politics spares no one.

OLDEST ELECTED OFFICIALS

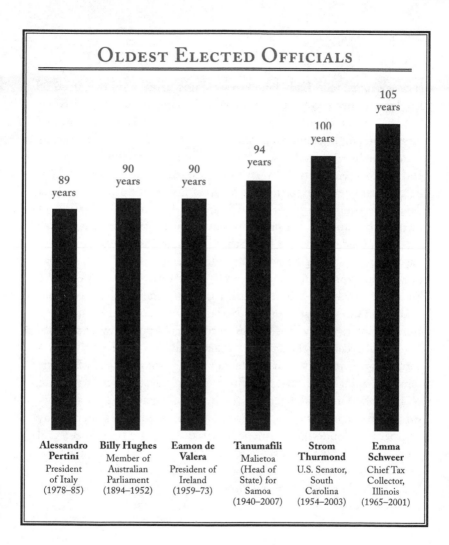

					105 years
				100 years	
			94 years		
89 years	90 years	90 years			
Alessandro Pertini	**Billy Hughes**	**Eamon de Valera**	**Tanumafili**	**Strom Thurmond**	**Emma Schweer**
President of Italy (1978–85)	Member of Australian Parliament (1894–1952)	President of Ireland (1959–73)	Malietoa (Head of State) for Samoa (1940–2007)	U.S. Senator, South Carolina (1954–2003)	Chief Tax Collector, Illinois (1965–2001)

TEEN QUEEN'S REIGN CUT SHORT

Inexperienced teen Lady Jane Grey's single distinction as Queen of England is her record as the shortest-serving monarch in British history. As the childless King Edward VI of England lay dying of tuberculosis in the summer of 1553, his longtime advisor, the ambitious Lord Northumberland, feared that the king's death would bring an end to his own political career. King Edward's eldest sister, Mary, held legitimate claim to the throne upon his death. But Mary was a devout Catholic, and Northumberland had gained his power and fortune by looting Catholic monasteries of their riches under Edward's predecessor. He knew that he would lose everything, perhaps even his life, if Mary or any other Catholic monarch rose to power. So Northumberland plotted to elevate to the throne the king's staunchly Protestant cousin, the shy, apolitical 16-year-old Lady Jane Grey. First, Northumberland convinced Jane's parents to compel Jane to marry his son, Guilford. Then, upon Edward's death, Northumberland tricked the reluctant Jane into participating in a coronation ceremony that made her Queen of England. But the scheme quickly unraveled when Mary escaped the ambush Northumberland had arranged for her. Mary gathered an army of supporters and headed back toward London. As her army approached London, Parliament declared Mary the true Queen and Jane a traitor. After just nine days of rule, Queen Jane was dethroned without so much as a battle. Jane, Guilford, and Northumberland were arrested, imprisoned, and eventually beheaded. **Political Lesson:** Be wary of getting drafted for office.

White House vs. Istana Nurul Iman

	White House	Istana Nurul Iman
Location	1600 Pennsylvania Avenue in Washington, D.C., the capital of the United States	Just outside Bandar Seri Begawan, the capital of Brunei
Purpose	Houses the U.S. president and his immediate family, plus office space for top members of the president's administration	Houses Brunei's head of state, the Sultan of Brunei and his family, and serves as office space for the nation's prime minister and all other top government officials
Time to Build	1792–1800 (reconstructions and additions continued until 1946)	1984
Style	Georgian	Islamic and Malay
Cost	$232,371	$1.4 billion
Number of Rooms	132 rooms (35 bathrooms)	1,788 rooms (257 bathrooms)
Square Feet	55,000	2,152,782
Dining Space	Accommodates up to 140 guests	Accommodates up to 4,000 guests
Elevators	3	18
Luxuries	Five full-time chefs, movie theater, putting green, bowling alley in basement	Air-conditioned stable for 200 horses; 1,500-seat mosque; 564 chandeliers

HOW TO KISS A DROOLING BABY

1 Take the baby from the parent.
Place your feet about hip-distance apart to increase balance. Fully extend your arms away from your body, locking your elbows to help maintain maximum distance. Grasp the baby firmly beneath the arms so she is facing you.

2 Get a good look.
Raise your arms so the baby's head is about six inches above your own. Smile broadly and look admiringly at her. Maintain visual contact with the baby's drool streams. Hold this position long enough to allow any high-flow drool to drip off her face and into the space between the two of you.

3 Kiss the baby.
Aim for a dry area of the baby's cheeks or chin. If all these areas are drooled on, kiss her on the forehead. Hold the position long enough to let your staff photographer and any nearby photojournalists snap a picture.

4 Return the baby to the parent.
As you hand the baby back to the parent, offer a compliment about the baby or ask the parent a friendly question about her to make it appear she has made a deep and positive impression on you. Thank the parent for having such a wonderful child and move on.

Arms fully extended

Six inches above head

Elbows locked

Accept.

Observe.

Forehead is dry

Kiss.

Return.

MEDIEVAL "HARLOTS" TAKE OVER ITALY'S CHURCH AND STATE

A 10th-century mother and daughter used sexual manipulation to politically control their country for three decades, ushering in an "Age of Harlots" and a particularly dark era of Europe's Dark Ages. In 901, Roman nobleman Theophylact I effectively seized political control of Rome, and for a time held immense power over the affairs of the city, including the power to appoint the next Roman Catholic pope. But Theophylact's wife, a former prostitute named Theodora, persuaded him to name her lover as Pope Sergius III in 904. After becoming pope, Sergius began an affair with Theodora's teenage daughter Marozia. In 910, Marozia used her influence and the lessons she learned from her mother to make her husband Alberic the new political ruler of Rome. Alberic ruled with such corruption and brutality that a mob literally chased him from the city. Undeterred, Marozia began an affair with the archbishop of Ravenna and helped him become Pope John X in 914. Sensing a threat to her power when the pope formed an alliance with the king of Italy, she countered by marrying the king's half-brother and archrival, Guido of Tuscany, in 924. Marozia convinced Guido to successfully attack Rome, seize control of its government, murder Pope John X, and replace him with Leo VI. He would be followed by another Marozia favorite, Stephen VIII, who was in turn followed by Pope John XI, Marozia's illegitimate 21-year-old son by Pope Sergius. When her husband, Guido, died in 929, Marozia married the king of Italy, her late husband's half-brother and archenemy. This last play was short-lived, as the king was deposed in a coup during the couple's wedding reception by Alberic II, Marozia's son by her first husband. Alberic II imprisoned Marozia until she died in 937, finally ending her seductive and, up till then, successful political career.

Political Lesson: Politics makes strange bedfellows.

HOW TO PRETEND YOU CARE

Act like You're Actually Listening

⭐ Lean toward the speaker.
Lean closer when a voter talks to you, as though you want to hear every word she says. If appropriate, emphasize your undivided attention through physical contact by grasping the voter's arm or putting your hand on her shoulder.

⭐ Mirror the voter's body language.
If you are face-to-face with the voter, mirror her posture and body language. This common sales technique makes it appear like you are listening intently.

⭐ Pause before responding.
After the voter has finished speaking, act as though you are digesting what you have just heard and are thinking about an answer, even if you already know exactly what you are going to say.

⭐ Address the speaker by name.
Establish a friendly rapport by using her first name. Ask her to remind you if you forgot her name or if she failed to tell you. If the voter holds an office or honorary title, use that instead of the first name. If the voter is a senior, call him or her by the last name prefaced by "Mr." or "Mrs." as a sign of respect.

Mirror the voter's posture and body language.

★ Mimic the voter's emotion.
If you appear to share the feelings of the voter, she will be more likely to believe that you have heard and appreciated what she has said to you. She will also be much more likely to believe what you say to her.

★ Integrate the voter's own words into your response.
The voter will hear familiar language and believe that you are engaged and on point.

★ Ask a question.
Pick out a key phrase from what the speaker just said and use it to construct a simple question to seem further interested. The voter's "Taxes are too high" becomes your question, "Have taxes become too much of a worry for you?"

★ Do not yawn, sigh, or roll your eyes.

APPEAR TO AGREE

★ Nod.
If a voter is expressing an opinion or telling you something positive, nod along as he speaks. Alternate between smiling and tightening your lips while nodding to avoid looking like you are nodding on autopilot.

★ Accentuate the positive.
If a voter expresses an opinion that you only partially agree with, focus on the part of his statement that you do agree with. Reiterate your support without discussing other aspects of the voter's statement.

Sidestep confrontation.

If a voter has staked out a position that you vigorously disagree with, respond with a noncommittal acknowledgment like, "I hear what you're saying" or "That's interesting. I'm glad you shared that." Clap the voter on the back and smile, then move on.

 If the voter insists on arguing, bring up a common belief or value that no one can dispute.

Relate your statement to the political process or patriotism, e.g.: "You and I are both patriots who want to do what's best for our country. That means we have to hear each other out and respect each other's opinions, then work together to solve the problem."

 Do not scowl, grimace, or curse.

Political Brief

Andrew Johnson was so drunk at his United States vice presidential inauguration in 1865 that outgoing Vice President Hannibal Hamlin had to nudge him several times during his acceptance speech to stop him from rambling, then help him walk from the podium back to his seat.

GODFATHER OF MODERN DEMOCRACY GETS WHACKED BY HIS OWN IDEALS

A hero for England's aristocratic class in their triumphant power struggle against King Henry III, Simon de Montfort insisted on dispersing power to the lower classes as well. In doing so, he became a pivotal figure in the development of democracy—and sealed his own doom. When his brother-in-law, King Henry III of England, refused to honor the power-sharing agreement he had signed with his country's aristocrats, Simon de Montfort organized an army of the disgruntled barons. In 1264, he attacked Henry's forces at Lewes and quickly defeated them, imprisoning the king along with his son, Prince Edward. But instead of trying to take Henry's place on the throne, Montfort redistributed political power to his fellow barons, insisting that the barons in turn distribute some of their newfound power to the working classes. Under Montfort's new form of government, each borough in England selected two representatives to take part in legislating the country's affairs, essentially creating Europe's first elected parliament. But Montfort's fellow aristocrats resented sharing power with the commoners as much as they resented King Henry for not sharing power with them—perhaps even more. Most of the barons soon re-allied with Henry, helping the king's son escape from prison and assemble a massive army to battle Montfort. Edward's forces ambushed Montfort at Evesham, where they disguised themselves as the army of Montfort's son. Surprised and vastly outnumbered, Montfort and the few barons who remained loyal to him staged a desperate uphill charge, but were quickly slaughtered. Montfort died of a stab wound to the back.

Political lesson: Stick to your core constituency.

Unpopular Popular Uprisings

Uprising	Where and When	Rebels
The Fiji Coup	Suva, Fiji; May 19–July 13, 2000	Fiji nationalists, led by bankrupt businessman George Speight
The Satsuma Rebellion	Japan; February–September of 1877	Samurai warriors angry over their loss of power, privilege, and status with the government's push to modernize Japan
Napper Tandy's Rebellion	County Donegal, Ireland; September 1798	A small group of Irish expatriates and French sympathizers led by James Napper Tandy
The Spartacist Uprising	Berlin, Germany; January 5–12, 1919	A few hundred anarchists and communists led by Rosa Luxembourg and Karl Liebknecht
The Parliamentary Democracy Party Revolt	Burma; 1970s	A few hundred armed rebels led by former Prime Minister U Nu, who claimed he remained the true Burmese leader since being deposed in a 1962 coup

Revolt	Result
Rebels seized the Parliament and held it for two months, along with three dozen hostages, including Prime Minister Mahendra Chaudray.	When no larger rebellion materialized, Speight abandoned Parliament, then was captured two weeks later and sentenced to life in prison for treason.
Tens of thousands of samurai attacked a government fort, but were met by hundreds of thousands of soldiers who eventually wiped them out using modern weaponry and military tactics.	Recalled fondly in many movies, the revolt was reviled by most Japanese, who had suffered centuries of oppression by the samurai and were glad to see them eradicated.
The rebels landed and took over a small village, where Tandy posted a proclamation for all Irish to join in his revolt against English rule.	Tandy wrote his proclamation in English, which none of the Gaelic-speaking Irish townspeople could read. After no one joined his revolt, Tandy got drunk in a pub, then sailed off with his men.
Rebels blockaded several streets in Berlin, calling for workers to join them in a nationwide strike and revolution to overthrow the German government.	The revolt stalled when its leaders began arguing among themselves about what to do next, then government forces attacked, killing most of the revolutionaries and their leaders.
U Nu and his rebels tried agitating a wider revolt to restore him to power through military exercises launched from Thailand, but few Burmese answered their call to join.	U Nu accepted an offer of peace from the Burmese government and took up teaching Buddhism.

CHINESE UPRISING REPLACES CORRUPT EMPEROR WITH SAME

Outraged by government corruption, greed, and ineptitude, farmers in 1st-century China staged a populist rebellion that took over the nation's government. But after only a few years of rule, another popular uprising unseated them when the farmers turned out to be even more corrupt, greedy, and inept than the regime they had replaced. By AD 17, farmers in China's northern provinces found themselves impoverished and starving due to the policies of Emperor Wang Mang. After the emperor raised their taxes amid their other difficulties, the farmers attacked government offices and forts, and the emperor sent his army to subdue them. The rebels, lacking uniforms, applied red liner to their eyebrows to distinguish themselves from government soldiers in battle. The army had difficulty putting down the rebellion and began to rob local peasants and pillage farms to raise funds, causing even more locals to join the rebels. The strengthened Red Eyebrow forces defeated the army, then marched on the capital of Chang'an and took over the government. With no experience in governance or large-scale fiscal management, the Red Eyebrows decided to raise money the same way Emperor Wang's army had—through robbery and pillaging. The country was quickly overtaken by an economic depression and famine. A new rebellion rose up to challenge the Red Eyebrow government. Under the leadership of Feng Yi, the rebels also colored their eyebrows red and defeated the confused Red Eyebrows in battle in AD 27. The triumphant rebels installed their own emperor and most of the Red Eyebrows returned to their farms. A few years later when some former Red Eyebrow leaders began plotting another rebellion, their neighbors informed the government and had them executed.

Political Lesson: Don't become your own worst nightmare.

THE DEFENESTRATIONS OF PRAGUE
THREE OCCASIONS WHEN THE CITY'S POLITICAL DECORUM AND SOME OF ITS POLITICIANS WENT OUT THE WINDOW

Date	July 30, 1419	September 24, 1483	May 23, 1618
Location	New Town Hall on Prague's Charles Square	Various government buildings around the city	Hradcany Castle, also known as Prague Castle
Who	The mayor and six members of the city council vs. a mob of Hussites—political and religious reformers drawn mostly from the lower class	The mayor and eight town aldermen vs. revolutionaries led by a group of radical Hussites known as Ultraquists	Members of the country's new Protestant aristocracy vs. recently appointed regional governors, who were hardline Catholics
Immediate Cause	After city authorities ignored their request to release some fellow Hussites on trial for treason, the mob stormed the town hall to free them by force	Violent celebration of the Ultraquists' successful overthrow of the city's government	The appointment of the Catholic Ferdinand II as head of the Holy Roman Empire, which included Prague, to replace Emperor Matthias, who had instituted a policy of religious freedom
Defenestration	The Hussite mob seized the mayor and city councilmen, then hurled them out windows onto spears held by other mob members who remained outside	The revolutionaries murdered the city officials in their offices, then flung them out their windows into the streets	The Protestants accused the two new governors of violating the region's religious freedom decrees and tossed them out of a window into a large pile of horse manure

HOW TO CONTINUE A BANKRUPT CAMPAIGN

SQUEEZE DONORS FOR EXTRA CASH

⭐ Flatter.
Establish special honorific titles and categories ("Heroes," "Angels," "My Special Friends") for especially generous donors. Encourage competition among donors to see who can "win" the competition for the highest donation.

⭐ Personalize.
Have your spouse and/or children accompany you to meeting with donors. Emphasize how your life dreams and family's future are on the line.

⭐ Frighten.
Remind the donor of all the terrible things that your opponent will do if she wins. Emphasize the dire consequences to your donor's self-interest and ideals.

SWEET TALK YOUR STAFF INTO WORKING FOR FREE

⭐ Flatter.
Give your staffers that stay new, important-sounding titles, such as "Director" or "Manager" of some aspect of your operation. Their eagerness to build their own résumés may outweigh their empty pay envelopes.

★ Personalize.

Have your spouse and/or children accompany you to meetings with your staff. Emphasize how your life dreams and family's future are on the line. Enlist relatives who will work for free to assist with various aspects of the campaign and foster the feeling of "family."

★ Frighten.

Remind your staff of all the terrible things that your opponent will do if he wins. Emphasize the dire consequences to your staff's self-interest and ideals. Point out the axiom that loyalty in politics is rewarded, and disloyalty is remembered.

GAIN FREE MEDIA COVERAGE

★ Do something photogenic.

Deliver a speech in an iconic natural, military, historic, or scenic location that voters associate with the nation's core values, achievements of previously successful politicians, or heroic acts of patriotism. These locations may often be used free of charge.

★ Do something confrontational.

Accuse your opponent of a crime or dangerous incompetence. The media feeds on controversy and conflict, authentic or manufactured. Make certain there is at least some factual basis for your charges.

Parachute into your next campaign stop.

★ Do something "unexpected."
Show up at one of your opponent's events. Spend a night in a homeless shelter. Help a farmer with his planting or harvest. Literally parachute into a campaign stop. Support a key theme of your campaign by doing an appealing and dramatic act. Be sure that journalists are notified of the unusual or spontaneous event well in advance.

EXPLOIT YOUR FINANCIAL WOES AS A CAMPAIGN ISSUE

★ Denounce the influence of money on politics.
Give speeches that criticize how the political process has been bought and sold by big money interests. Call for a new campaign system that eliminates the influence money. Say it's time the government was returned to the people.

★ Audit your opponent.
Research the individuals, companies, and organizations that have contributed to your opponent's campaign. Assert, and denounce, the possibility that your opponent has been "bought and sold" by whatever and whomever these donors might be construed to represent—so long as these groups or individuals are not likely to contribute to your campaign. Highlighting an "us versus them" campaign, with "them" representing those not likely to donate to your campaign, will drive "us" donors to contribute in greater numbers and more generous amounts.

HOW TO HANDLE GETTING HIT WITH A PIE IN THE FACE

1 Close your eyes.

2 Shut your mouth.

3 Hold your ground.
Running away can make you look silly.

4 Make a joke.
Undermine the pie-thrower's attempt to make you angry or flustered. Show good humor and offer a joke such as, "But I ordered pecan—and only one slice."

5 Taste it.
Clear the pie from your eyes and give it a taste. Then offer another joke such as, "Not enough nutmeg."

6 Clean up.
Wipe your face with a towel dampened from a water bottle. Clear any pie out of your hair. Do not go to a restroom to wash up.

7 Stay in front of the cameras and show calm control over the situation.

Be mentally prepared to be hit by a pie in the face at any moment.

8 | Take off some clothes.
Remove pie-covered jacket, tie, or scarf. Do not remove shirt, pants, or skirt, except in private.

9 | Resume your activities.
A quick return to what you were doing before getting hit by the pie is essential to assuring voters you weren't unnerved by the attack.

Political Brief

At a May 2007 meeting of the Tainan City Council in Taiwan, Council member Liu Yin-chang rose and hurled a cup of feces onto his colleague Hsieh Lung-chieh. Liu, a member of the city's ruling Democratic Progressive Party, said he was retaliating against the rival Kuomintang Party's Hsieh for accusing him of being a dirty politician in the recent election campaign. Tainan City Council Speaker Huang Yu-wen ordered Liu to leave the building and called for a recess. The Kuomintang councilors left the building in protest and filed criminal charges and a lawsuit against Liu, who was suspended from his political party and the Tainan City Council for the remainder of his term.

POLITICAL BEANBALL
POLITICIANS AND THE THINGS PEOPLE THROW AT THEM

Who	Hit With	Thrown By	Why?
Tony Blair, Prime Minister of England 1997–2007	Eggs	Two fathers	To protest changes in child custody laws
Eva Perón, First Lady of Argentina 1946–52	Tomatoes	Group of Swiss citizens	To protest her arrival in Switzerland
Dan Glickman, U.S. Secretary of Agriculture 1995–2001	Bison entrails	Native American environmental activist	To protest federal government's bison policies
Bettino Craxi Prime Minister of Italy 1983–87	Coins	Students shouting, "Bettino, do you want these, too?"	To protest corruption scandal in which Craxi was alleged to have stolen millions

BORIS NIKOLAYEVICH YELTSIN

Russian President, Famous Drunk

WORST DEEDS: A long series of embarrassing incidents brought on by his excessive drinking and buffoonery, including: goosing a secretary during a Kremlin office photo shoot • throwing a woman off a dock into the Red Sea during a photo op • going for a late-night drunken drive and winter swim in the Potomac River on a 1993 diplomatic trip to the United States • challenging a group of journalists who had asked him about his declining health to compete against him in swimming, tennis, and track and field events • berating a weary Pope John Paul II to "sit back down" when he tried to excuse himself from a Vatican function with Yeltsin, then later expressing his "boundless love for Italian women" during a dinner toast

BORN: February 1, 1931, in the village of Butko in the Sverdlovsk Province of Russia, where he was almost drowned in his baptismal font by a drunken priest

DIED: April 23, 2007, in Moscow, Russia

NICKNAME: Ole Lukoye (after an evil, demented dwarf)

QUOTE: "I can honestly tell you, I just overslept. The security services did not let in the people who were due to wake me. Of course, I will sort things out and punish them." —Yeltsin, after getting so drunk on a 1994 flight from the United States to Ireland that he passed out and failed to wake up to get off the plane for a scheduled meeting with Irish Premier Albert Reynolds

MISSING IN ACTION

Politician	Supposed to be in	Was actually in	Absence
Richard William Butler, Governor of Tasmania 2003–04	Tasmania	Various vacation spots around southeast Asia	3 weeks
Ibrahim Rugova President of Kosovo 1992–2006	Kosovo	Italy	3 months
Henry VI King of England 1422–61; 1470–71	An insane asylum; Scotland	London, England	First absence was 14 months; second lasted 9 years
Richard I King of England 1189–99	England	The Middle East and France	9.5 years (out of his 10-year reign)
Demetrius II King of Syria 147–125 BC	Syria	Iran	10 years
Alexander III (the Great) King of Macedon 336–323 BC	Pella, Macedon	Egypt, India, Afghanistan, Iran	11 years

HOW TO SIMULATE SOBRIETY

★ Move in a circuitous path.
Avoid trying to move in a straight line. Circle, stop, start, and veer purposefully.

★ Limit interactions.
Do not attempt long or complicated explanations. Offer short answers to questions, and keep encounters brief. Designate a staff member to keep you moving, and to apologize that your tight schedule requires you to hurry.

★ Resize your eyes.
Use eye drops to contract your pupils, which will be dilated when you are under the influence. Apply the drops in private.

★ Steer clear of passion.
Intoxicants loosen inhibitions. Keep your distance from people you strongly dislike or to whom you are sexually attracted.

Be Aware
Clear alcohols like vodka and gin leave a fainter odor on the breath than darker alcohols, such as beer and whiskey. Keep mints or a small bottle of mouthwash handy to mask any lingering odor.

Avoid trying to move in a straight line.

I HAVE A LIST

HOW TO COUNTER A SMEAR AD

IF THE AD IS TRUE OR WOULD BE DIFFICULT TO DISPROVE

★ Denounce your opponent for dragging the campaign into the mud.

★ Remind voters of all the important issues involved in the campaign.

★ Emphasize that voters deserve better.
Tell voters they need candidates and leaders who offer hopes and solutions, not negativity and partisanship.

★ Promise to stay on the high road for the rest of campaign and invite voters along for the ride.

★ Encourage supporters to produce an ad showing your opponent to be guilty of a more serious offense.

IF THE ATTACK AD IS ONLY PARTIALLY TRUE

★ Craft a deflecting response.
Focus on the attack ad's inaccuracies and exaggerations.

★ Point out how your opponent is guilty of twisting the truth.
Claim that your opponent's trustworthiness is now an issue.

*Produce an ad showing your opponent
to be guilty of a more serious offense.*

Assert that the ad takes what you said or did out of context.

 Demand that your opponent apologize and withdraw the ad. If he refuses, cite that as proof that your opponent is unwilling to admit and correct his mistakes and would therefore make a poor leader.

IF THE AD IS COMPLETELY UNTRUE AND CAN EASILY BE PROVEN FALSE

 Denounce the ad as completely untrue.
Say you are not going to dignify the charges by responding.

 Use reporters to make your case.
Encourage them to look into the matter and write stories. Remind them of unscrupulous politicians who engaged in similar defamatory practices and the damage they did. Stories by objective journalists calling the attack ad false will be much more effective than any response from your campaign.

 Recruit respected elder statesmen and community leaders to denounce your opponent for the slander.

 Give the disproven allegations a name.
For the rest of the campaign, refer to "sweater-gate" (or whatever you name the charges) and how it demonstrates your opponent's mistakes and unsuitability for office. Be sure the tide has turned completely in your favor before you again raise the allegations.

Be Aware

Watch out for a rival's tracker, who might be video-taping your every move. A tracker will follow you the entire campaign to tape every public appearance you make hoping to catch an inconsistency or even more embarrassing lapse.

WORST POLITICAL NICKNAMES

Politician	Position	Nickname
Lugaid mac Con	King of Ireland AD 195–225	"The Dog's Son"
Louis V	King of France 966–87	"Louis the Sluggard"; also "The Coward King"
Alfonso IX	King of León 1188–1230	"The Slobberer"
Mustafa I	Sultan of Ottoman Empire 1617–18, 1622–23	"The Fake"
Pierre Elliott Trudeau	Prime Minister of Canada 1968–79, 1980–84	"Lil' Fart"
Margaret Thatcher	Prime Minister of England 1979–90	"The Milk Snatcher"
Ramon Ravilla Jr.	Governor of Philippine province of Cavite 1998–2004	"Bong"
John Edwards	U.S. Senator (1998–2004); Democratic Nominee for Vice President (2004)	"The Breck Shampoo Girl"

POLITICAL STRATEGIST FINDS WISDOM AND REDEMPTION, LOSES LIFE AND AUDIENCE

The leading American campaign strategist of his generation, Republican political operative Lee Atwater collapsed during a 1990 speech at a Republican fundraising breakfast. Atwater began twitching uncontrollably in the middle of a joke about how he had made Democrat Michael Dukakis look like Rocky the Flying Squirrel in an attack ad he had launched during the previous presidential election. He then screamed and fell over. Atwater was rushed to a nearby hospital where he was diagnosed with an inoperable brain tumor. Atwater's attack ads and whisper campaigns had helped George Bush Sr. overcome Dukakis's big early lead to easily win the United States presidency in 1992. Atwater's "Rocky the Squirrel" ad was a 30-second video of Dukakis wearing an ill-fitting helmet riding around in a tank during a photo op, looking uncomfortable and out of place. The imagery helped raise voter concerns about the ability of Dukakis, who had no foreign policy or national political experience, to lead the country's military. After collapsing and being told he had only a few months to live, Atwater underwent a religious and political conversion. He apologized to his political victims, including Dukakis. Atwater also wrote essays for national magazines denouncing the moral decay in American politics and society brought on by the brand of dirty politics that he had practiced so successfully. He died in March of 1991. One of Atwater's pupils, Karl Rove, went on to run the presidential campaigns of Bush's son George W. Bush in 2000 and 2004, successfully applying and escalating his brand of campaigning while ignoring Atwater's late-life advice for a more civil political discourse.

Political Lesson: People will do as you did, not as you said.

Prime Slimes
Infamous Attack Ads

Campaign	Target	Point of Attack	Attack
1806 Dutch Campaign to Maintain Independence	Louis Bonaparte	Rumors that Napoleon Bonaparte meant to place his brother Louis on the Dutch throne	"An Appeal to the Batavian People," a pamphlet warning that Louis's rule would lead to economic ruin and slavery for the Dutch people
1964 U.S. Presidential Race	Barry Goldwater, Republican Party nominee	Goldwater's support for using nuclear weapons in the Vietnam War	TV ad depicting a young girl picking daisies, then spotting a nearby nuclear bomb blast
2000 U.S. Senate Race in Montana	Mike Taylor, Republican nominee	Taylor, a rancher, had owned and operated a hairdressing school in Colorado in the 1970s	TV ad with disco soundtrack and archival footage of a bushy-haired Taylor massaging hair care products into men's scalps
1993 Canadian Federal Elections	Jean Chrétien, head of Liberal Party	Chrétien's face, half-paralyzed due to Bell's Palsy	TV ad showing unflattering pictures of Chrétien's deformity interspersed with video of actors posing as regular Canadians saying they would be ashamed to have Chrétien as their prime minister
2005 New Zealand Parliamentary	Labor Party leader Helen Clark	Rumors about the sexual orientation of Clark	A cartoon on the National Party Web site depicting Clark as Darth Vader revealing to Luke Skywalker, "Luke, I am your lesbian father."

PRANKSTER TARGETS, TEACHES NIXON

Democratic prankster Dick Tuck began tormenting Richard M. Nixon in California in 1950 when he became a mole on Nixon's successful United States Senate campaign. When Nixon unsuccessfully sought the presidency ten years later, his opponent John F. Kennedy hired Tuck to play practical jokes on Nixon. The day after the first candidates' debate—a contest many felt Nixon had won—Tuck spun the results by hiring an elderly woman wearing a Nixon button to hug Nixon in front of reporters and console him for losing the debate. Two years later when Nixon ran for governor of California, Tuck had children in Los Angeles's Chinatown greet him with a sign reading "Welcome Nixon" in English and beneath the greeting "What about the Hughes loan?" in Chinese—a reference to a controversial loan Nixon's brother received. Nixon, who did not understand Chinese, posed smiling next to the sign, then tore it up in front of reporters when Tuck told him the translation. During a whistle-stop train tour on the same campaign, Tuck disguised himself as a conductor and ordered Nixon's train to pull away from the station just as Nixon had begun a speech to a crowd. When Nixon ran for president in 1968, Tuck hired pregnant women to show up at his rallies wearing T-shirts that read "Nixon's the One." Nixon, who had mastered the art of overt dirty tricks early in his career, came to both despise and begrudgingly admire Tuck. During his 1972 presidential reelection campaign, Nixon ordered aides to develop a "Dick Tuck capability." Nixon's staffers and operatives initiated a series of covert dirty tricks, culminating in the break-in of Democratic headquarters in the Watergate building. The burglars were caught and the subsequent Watergate scandal forced the disgraced Nixon to resign from office two years later.

Political Lesson: Be careful whom you imitate.

HOW TO SNIFF OUT AND CO-OPT A MOLE

1   Keep your suspicions to yourself.
Do not let your staffers know that you suspect anyone on the team of disloyalty in leaking information. Instilling your staff with a sense of distrust can do greater damage to the campaign than a mole, and will definitely send the mole underground, covering his tracks.

2   Perform a leak audit.
Create a two-column chart with the leaks on one side and the names of people who had access to the information before it was leaked on the other. The names that appear next to multiple leaks are your prime mole suspects.

3   Follow the trail.
If none of the people who had access to the leaked information turns out to be the mole, make a list of people who may have gained information from them—assistants, love interests, relatives, personal trainers, babysitters, dog walkers, etc. Loyal staffers may sometimes inadvertently pass on information to moles inside the campaign or to people in the outside world. Moles often prefer to leak information they learn second-hand because it keeps them a step removed from direct suspicion.

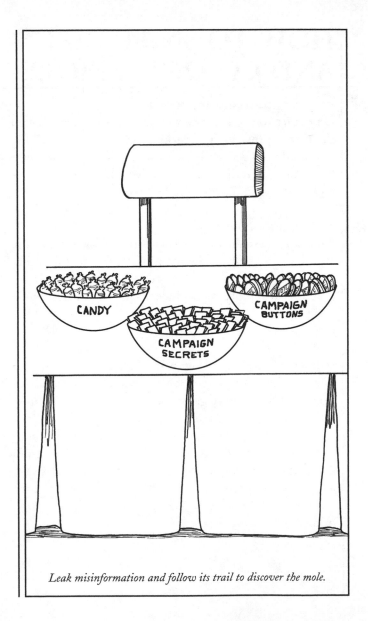

Leak misinformation and follow its trail to discover the mole.

4 | Plant bad information.
Once you have a prime suspect, divulge a probably false but seemingly damning bit of information about yourself in a way that allows the mole to think that she has received the information without you noticing (for example, allow the mole to overhear a fake phone conversation). If that false information turns up in the media or as part of a rival's attack on you, you've identified the mole. To smoke out multiple mole suspects, plant slightly different false information with each.

5 | Do not reveal the mole.
Resist the urge to confront the mole or reveal his identity to other staffers. Flushing the mole from hiding will only encourage your opponents to attempt to plant a replacement mole whose identity you will then have to determine.

6 | Use the mole to your advantage.
Knowing the identity of a mole on your staff provides you with a potentially valuable resource. Use the mole to leak misinformation such as false position papers or advertising plans or financial details that your opposition will then waste time and money adjusting to. Your opponent might even attack you for holding one of these phantom positions or policies, giving you the opportunity to demonstrate the inaccuracies and untrustworthiness of your opponent's claims.

ALCIBIADES

Athenian Statesman and General

WORST DEEDS: Causing the end of the Golden Age of Athens ★ Convincing Athens to restart a war against Sparta, then defecting to Sparta during his first military expedition ★ Leading the Spartans to a series of victories over his former Athenian countrymen ★ Being exiled from Sparta after seducing and impregnating the Spartan King's wife, then insisting that the child be named in his honor ★ Enlisting Persia's help in a series of plots against Sparta ★ Masterminding a coup to overthrow the democratic government of Athens ★ Conspiring to overthrow his fellow coup leaders to install himself at a high rank in the Athenian government and military ★ Leading Athens back to battle against his former comrades in Sparta, then abandoning them after early losses ★ Winning many of his most famous military victories through trickery rather than battle ★ Cutting off the tail of his favorite pet dog in order to amuse himself with the subsequent criticism by his neighbors

BORN: 450 BC in Athens, Greece

DIED: Assassinated by Spartan soldiers in 404 BC after attempting to incite the people of Phrygia to attack Sparta

NICKNAME: The Chameleon

EDUCATION: Studied for a time under Socrates, who failed to convert him to a more virtuous life

FIRST JOB: Athenian diplomat

QUOTE: "His habits offended everyone and caused them to commit affairs to other hands and, thus, before long to ruin the city." — Thucydides, Athenian aristocrat and historian

ODD POLITICAL ADVISERS

Politician	Adviser	Advising Method
Wu Ding Head of China's Shang Dynasty 1250–1192 BC	Oracle bones— the shoulder blades of oxen	Bones were heated until they broke, then cracks were read to determine future courses of action
Lycurgus Regent of Sparta 7th century BC	Pythia, the Oracle at Delphi	Gazed into pungent mists wafting up through a fissure in rocks for inspiration
Julius Caesar Ruler of Rome 49–44 BC	Titus Vestricius Spurinna, an Etruscan Haruspex	Cut open animals and "read" their entrails
Nicholas II Czar of Russia 1894–1917	Grigori Rasputin	Gained visions after engaging in excessive alcohol consumption and sexual orgies
Alfred Deakin Australian Prime Minister 1903–10	Ghosts of former prime ministers	Summoned the ghosts of the home's former residents to ask advice on government policy
Bill Clinton U.S. President 1993–2001	Tony Robbins	Used technique of neuro-associative conditioning to "reprogram" a client's brain to overcome fears and achieve success
Frank Hsieh Premier of Republic of China 2005–06	Sung Chi-li	Used Photoshopped pictures showing bright beams emanating from his head to claim he was a supernatural being who regularly left his body to gain insight on the future

TOO MUCH DEFENSE LEADS TO DEMISE OF PERSIAN EMPEROR

Aazar e Narsi headed the Persian Empire's Sassanid Dynasty for only three months during AD 302, but he still managed to almost bankrupt the kingdom by indulging his vices and attempting to kill nearly all his enemies, friends, staff, and family. When he tried to murder his pregnant sister-in-law after envisioning her giving birth to his successor, Narsi's bodyguards concluded their monarch had finally gone too far. The guards took Narsi's sword and decapitated him with it, then placed his crown on his sister-in-law's swollen belly—history's only recorded prenatal coronation. Born later that year, the child was named King Shahpour after the renowned Persian emperor from the previous century who had defeated the Romans in battle and brought on the dynasty's first golden age. Shahpour II ably led the empire for 70 years in what is regarded as the second golden age of the Sassanid Dynasty.

Political Lesson: Try to get along with someone.

Political Brief

In 1978, San Francisco City Supervisor Dan White resigned, but changed his mind a few weeks later and asked Mayor George Moscone to re-appoint him. After Moscone refused, White shot him in City Hall, then killed City Supervisor Harvey Milk. During his trial, White argued that he did not premeditate the crimes and offered his depression and excessive consumption of Twinkies and junk food as evidence that he could not have premeditated the murders. The jury agreed and convicted him of only manslaughter.

SHOULD HAVE CHECKED REFERENCES
KILLED BY THEIR OWN STAFFERS

Leader	Homicidal Staffer	Method	Reason
Galba Roman Emperor AD 68–69	His Praetorian bodyguards	Lynched	Was late paying their wages
Pertinax Roman Emperor AD 192–93	His Praetorian bodyguards	Stabbed in the back	Only paid them half of their wages
Constantine the Bearded Byzantine Emperor AD 641–668	His head housekeeper	Stabbed while taking bath	Discontent over his plan to move the empire's capital
Agha Mohammad Khan Shah of Persia 1794–97	Three domestic servants	Stabbed in bed as he slept	Feared Khan would behead them when he found out they had eaten a slice of melon he intended to have for breakfast
Park Chung-hee President of South Korea 1963–78	Kim Jaeguy, director of Korea's intelligence agency	Invited the president to a crowded *private* dinner and shot him	Felt Park had become too dictatorial
Alsan Maskhadov President of Chechnya 1997–2005	Bodyguard	Accidental shooting	Gun misfired while he was loading it to defend Maskhadov's bunker from attack by Russian special forces

LOST LETTER CAUSES AFRICAN RULER TO LOSE HIS KINGDOM AND HIS LIFE

Looking to save his country from takeover, King Tewodros II of Ethiopia reached out to his old friend Queen Victoria of England. A longtime Christian stronghold, Ethiopia enjoyed warm relations with England, but the country's religious preferences irked the Muslims to the north in Egypt and northeastern Africa. With a Muslim invasion of Ethiopia seeming imminent, Tewodros sent a letter in 1862 asking Queen Victoria to send British military instructors to come teach his army to manufacture and handle firearms. Tewodros entrusted the letter's delivery to British consul Charles Duncan Cameron, but Cameron's superiors sent him on a series of diplomatic missions, including to Egypt, and had him forward rather than deliver the letter to England. When Tewodros' letter arrived in London, it was misplaced for over a year, then sent to the British Foreign Office in India, where it languished for another year. Thinking the Queen had snubbed him, and hearing that Cameron had gone to visit his antagonistic Muslim neighbors right after he had been entrusted with the letter, Tewodros assumed that he had been double-crossed. He took Cameron and the rest of the British embassy hostage in a desperate effort to finally gain Queen Victoria's attention. The British responded by invading Ethiopia and quickly overwhelming the Ethiopian soldiers, most of whom did not have guns. Determined to avoid the humiliation of capture, Tewodros shot himself to death with one of the few guns in the country, a pistol sent to him years before as a gift by Queen Victoria of England.

Political Lesson: Check your assumptions before acting.

PAUL KEATING

Prime Minister of Australia

WORST DEEDS: Creating controversy after touching Queen Elizabeth II in an inappropriate manner during her 1982 visit to Australia, then responding, "I like the Queen...and I think she liked me." ★ Referring to Malaysian Prime Minister Dr. Mahathir bin Mohamad as a "recalcitrant," angering Mahathir into canceling billions of dollars of trade deals between Malaysia and Australia ★ Informing his wife of 23 years, Anita, that he wanted a divorce during a friend's dinner party ★ Referring to rival parties during Parliamentary debate, interviews, and other public events, as: "pansies," "clowns," "scumbags," "frauds," "dummies and dimwits," "desperadoes," "intellectual hoboes," "irrelevant, useless, and immoral," "mangy maggots," "cowards and hillbillies," and "a bunch of nobodies going nowhere" ★ Referring to rival individual members of Parliament as a: "pig," "boxhead," "Old Jellyback," "the brain-damaged leader of the Opposition," "stupid, foul mouthed grub," "an intellectual rust bucket," "a gutless spiv," "the poor, old thing," "a painted, perfumed gigolo," "this piece of vermin," "a political carcass with a coat and tie on," "some pumped up bunyip potentate," "the Shrek," "an Easter Island statue with its arse full of razor blades," "a complete political harlot," "an abacus gone feral," and "a dog returning to his vomit"

BORN: January 18, 1944

EDUCATION: De La Salle College in Bankstown

FIRST JOB: Clerk for a trade union

QUOTE: "Paul Keating is an unguided missile." —Australian Workplace Relations Minister Joe Hockey, after Keating likened the policies of Hockey's colleague John Howard to those of Adolf Hitler

POLITICAL CRITTERS
ANIMALS WHO INFLUENCED POLITICS

Critters	Action	Impact
The Canine Kings of Ptremphanae	Served as rulers of the African kingdom	Guided governmental policy by either wagging their tails in approval, growling to show hostility, or exhibiting indifference to proposals by their ministers
An asp	Bit and killed Cleopatra VII in 31 BC as she held the snake to her chest in an act of suicide	Ended the long line of Egyptian pharaohs ruling Egypt as well as the Roman Civil War between Caesar, Cleopatra, and Marc Antony
Genghis Khan's horse	Threw off Khan in 1227, mortally wounding the ruler of the vast Mongol Empire	Set off a battle of succession that temporarily stalled Mongol expansion
Pet fox	Bit its owner Charles Lennox, governor of Upper Canada (1818–19), infecting him with rabies	Lennox died within a few months from rabies, probably delaying by decades the eventual union of Upper and Lower Canada
Rats in Washington, D.C.'s National Hotel	Drowned in hotel's vats of cooking water, infecting food served at President James Buchanan's 1857 inaugural dinner	Killed dozens of dinner guests and sickened Buchanan so badly he had to spend the first few weeks of his presidency in bed
Humphrey the cat	Named official "Mouser" to the Cabinet Office in 1989 by British Prime Minister Margaret Thatcher	Saved British government thousands of dollars in extermination fees each year. Later set off scandal when he was accused of wiping out a nest of baby robins

CALIGULA INDULGES HIS FAVORITE STALLION, GETS BUCKED OFF ROMAN THRONE

During his reign as Roman emperor from AD 37–41, Caligula positioned his horse Incitatus as a member of the Roman senate. The appointment to Rome's top legislative body represented another in a long line of honors Caligula bestowed upon his favorite animal. The Spanish white stallion wore a jeweled necklace and blankets of imperial purple—a color reserved by Roman law for royalty. Incitatus drank from an ivory trough and lived in a marble stable the size of a palace attended by over a dozen servants. Caligula hosted Incitatus at his own royal palace as an honored guest for many of his dinner parties, where the horse's feed was supplemented with gold flakes. Caligula, who was fond of performing grand stunts to prove his power, chose Incitatus to accompany him on one of his most brazen endeavors. Thrasyllus, the soothsayer of his predecessor Tiberius, had once predicted that Caligula had as much chance of becoming emperor as he did of riding a horse over the Bay of Naples. So in AD 39, Caligula had a temporary bridge of rafts and boats stretched across the bay from the towns of Puteoli to Baiae, and rode Incitatus from boat to boat across the three-mile stretch. When Incitatus died the following year, he received a lavish funeral and parade through the streets of Rome, with Caligula ordering his subjects to venerate the horse as a god. Caligula's doting on Incitatus helped convince those around him that he was either too arrogant or insane to remain in office. Caligula's bodyguards conspired with some senators and assassinated him in AD 41.

Political Lesson: You make enemies when you treat your friends too well.

STRANGE PETS OF WORLD LEADERS

Orangutan
Josephine
Empress of France (1804–14)

Giraffe
Julius Caesar
Ruler of Rome (49–44 BC)

A rat named "Jonathan"
Teddy Roosevelt
U.S. President (1901–09)

A hippo named "Billy"
Calvin Coolidge
U.S. President (1923–29)

Porcupine
Louis IX
King of France (1226–70)

Alligator (kept in bathtub
at White House)
John Quincy Adams
U.S. President (1825–29)

Leopard
Mobutu Sese Seko
President of Zaire (1965–97)

Elephant
Charlemagne
Holy Roman Emperor (800–14)

HOW TO WORK A HOSTILE ROOM

1 Plan quick exit routes.

When making an appearance in front of an organization or in a locale that is traditionally hostile to you or
your party, immediately assess your closest routes of
entry and exit. Note areas where you may be confronted
by protesters, or any open public areas from which you
might be struck by tomatoes, eggs, pies, or other
thrown objects. During the event, ensure that staffers
are positioned to be able to clear a quick means of
escape, and are peripherally located to watch for
hurled projectiles.

2 Humanize yourself.

Arrive early and engage with individuals and small
groups of two or three. Try to connect on a personal
level, discussing family, hobbies, sports, the weather, or
other nonpolitical subjects to try to humanize yourself
and temper hostility that would be directed at you during
the event itself.

3 Arrange an introduction.

Have your staff arrange for a respected local figure
to introduce your address to the group. After the
introduction, praise the person's achievements and
character—applaud the speaker and urge the crowd
to join you.

Surround yourself with children.

4 Extend praise and work common ground.

Emphasize your common belief in basic concepts shared by virtually everyone. Compliment the audience and the citizens of the city, state, province, territory, or country for safely assumed truisms such as dedication to family, security, and prosperity, and avow that you share these values. Declare your opposition to crime, poverty, illness, unhappiness, and other things generally understood to be bad. Avoid specifics.

5 Acknowledge and isolate differences.

Acknowledge issues of disagreement by saying that being able to point to a difference of opinion openly is the first important step to finding agreement, and express your interest in coming to such agreement. Avoid specifics.

6 Surround yourself with children.

Bring a group of local children to the event, preferably from disadvantaged backgrounds. Mention them during your speech as examples of "the future." If the event becomes heated or confrontational, summon the children to gather around you and ask the crowd to maintain calm and civility "for the sake of the children." Note that the presence of children also reduces your chance of being the target of thrown objects.

7 Exit the event as soon as possible.

Wildest Legislative Brawls

Where and When	Combatants
Floor of South Korean National Assembly December 2007	Members of the ruling United New Democratic Party vs. members of the opposition Grand National Party
Floor of Senate of Australian Parliament December 2003	Democratic Senator Andrew Bartlett vs. Liberal Senator Jeannie Ferris
Lunch meeting in conference hall of Taiwan's Legislative Yuan October 2004	Members of the opposition Nationalist Party vs. members of the ruling Progressive Party
Floor of U.S. Senate May 1856	Senator Charles Sumner of Massachusetts vs. U.S. Representative Preston Brooks of South Carolina
Mexico's Congress November 2006	Legislators of the opposition Democratic Revolution Party (PRD) vs. members of the ruling National Action Party (PAN)
Sri Lankan Parliament July 2004	Legislators from rival parties

Why	Brawl
Debate over a bill to impeach prosecutors who cleared a GNP presidential candidate of involvement in a fraud case	As the UNDP tried to clear the podium to submit the bill, opposition GNP legislators barricaded the podium with chains, metal bars, and sofas, while lawmakers from the UNDP tried to break through the barricade using power saws.
Just after a legislative vote, Bartlett confronted Ferris over her staffers taking back five bottles of wine Bartlett had stolen from a Christmas gala earlier in the day	Bartlett cursed at Ferris, then grabbed her arm. When Ferris fled the senate chamber, Bartlett chased after her, screaming more abuse.
Heated debate over international arms sales	An anonymous Progressive hurled a hard-boiled egg at Nationalist Chu Fong-chi, who ducked then dumped her entire lunch onto the Progressives' Chen Chong-yi, setting off a lengthy food fight involving dozens of legislators.
During a senate speech the previous day, Sumner accused Brooks's nephew Senator Andrew Butler of being a "pimp for slavery"	Brooks beat Sumner with his gold-tipped walking cane. When Sumner hid under his desk, Brooks ripped it off the floor and continued beating Sumner until he passed out from head trauma and loss of blood.
Outraged by election irregularities, PRD members vowed not to let incoming President Felipe Calderon take his oath of office	PAN members seized control of the floor by force and would not yield despite three days of off-and-on fighting.
Charges that Sri Lankan Prime Minister Chandrika Kumaratunga carried a bomb in her purse to a cabinet meeting	Legislators battled for almost an hour, much of the fighting taking place around the ceremonial mace, which opposition legislators tried to grab to use as a weapon. One legislator—a Buddhist monk—had to be hospitalized after the fight.

AFGHAN TRANSPORTATION REFORMER KILLED BY MOB DEMANDING TRANSPORTATION REFORM

When the Taliban government fell in 2001, Abdul Rahman returned to Afghanistan to become the Aviation and Transportation Minister. Rahman wanted to play an active role in rebuilding his native country, which had been devastated by years of Taliban rule. A political reformer, medical doctor, and strong believer in democracy and free markets, Rahman felt he could improve his country's image and turn Afghanistan into a popular tourist destination if he modernized its transportation infrastructure. On February 14, 2002, Rahman went to the Kabul airport to catch a flight for an official visit to New Delhi. The airport was crowded with hundreds of angry Haj pilgrims who had been stranded for days by flight delays and cancellations on their way to Mecca. Rahman drove past the pilgrims waiting in the terminal and boarded a government jet sitting on the runway. The outraged pilgrims formed a mob and ran out to the runway. They surrounded Rahman's plane and prevented it from taking off. The mob demanded an explanation for why their flights to fulfill a religious duty had been held up while his government flight had been expedited. When Rahman emerged from the plane to try to reason with the angry travelers, the mob seized him and beat him to death. They tossed Rahman's bloody body onto the runway and returned to the airport terminal to await their flights.

Political Lesson: Do not try and reason with an angry mob.

MOB HITS
POLITICIANS KILLED BY CROWDS

Who	Mob	Means
Filiberto Lopez Perez Mayor of Chanal, Mexico, 1991	Hundreds of his constituents, enraged that he had banned the sale of liquor	Beaten to death over the course of two hours
Benito Mussolini Italian Dictator, 1922–43	Dozens of Communist partisans	Seized while trying to escape Italy disguised as a German soldier; shot and hung on a meat hook in Milan's town square
Joseph Smith Jr. U.S. Presidential Candidate (1844); Founder of the Church of Jesus Christ of Latter-Day Saints	200 men outraged by rumors that Smith intended to establish a polygamist kingdom in Illinois	Shot three times, fell from a second-story window to the street, then propped against a wall and shot repeatedly
Johann de Witt Leader of Holland, 1653–72	Protestant lynch mob angered by his failed international policies	Ambushed while visiting his brother in jail, de Witt was dragged into the street where he and his brother were shot, hung, and partially eaten
Robert Imbrie U.S. Consul in Iran, 1924	Religious zealots outraged that Imbrie had taken a photograph of one of their sacred shrines	Beaten and stabbed to death
Cleander Head of Rome's Praetorian Guard and Top Adviser to Emperor Commodus, 190 BC	Hundreds of Roman peasants rioting over food shortages, later joined by legion soldiers	Chased into a Roman royal palace by the mob of peasants, who then demanded that Commodus decapitate him and present them with his head

CASSIUS MARCELLUS CLAY MAKES HIS ATTACKERS SUFFER

Cassius Marcellus Clay, a United States antislavery activist, proved so enraging to proslavery forces in pre–Civil War Kentucky, they hired political enforcer Sam Brown to assassinate him. Brown shot Clay in the chest at a political debate in 1843. The large and ferocious Clay, who once frightened a rival into committing suicide the night before they were to meet in a duel, responded by pulling his Bowie knife. Despite having a bullet in his chest and being restrained by Brown's allies, Clay managed to cut off Brown's nose and left ear and gouge out his right eye. He then picked up Brown and tossed him over a wall and down an embankment. Clay's counterattack on Brown seemed so extreme he was arrested for mayhem. Clay was assaulted again six years later after making another speech calling for slave emancipation. Cyrus Turner, son of a proslavery politician, and his five brothers surrounded Clay, punching and clubbing him repeatedly. They took away Clay's Bowie knife and stabbed him several times with it. One brother put a pistol to Clay's head, but the gun kept misfiring. As he was about to be stabbed again, Clay took back his knife, scattering his attackers. He then chased down Cyrus Turner and stabbed him to death before passing out from his wounds. Clay recovered and went on to serve under President Lincoln as an ambassador to Russia, where he convinced his hosts to send their Navy to support the North in the U.S. Civil War and to sell Alaska to the United States in 1867. At the age of 92, Clay took on three assailants who broke into his home at night, shooting one to death, disemboweling another with his Bowie knife, and seriously wounding the third. Clay died the following year of natural causes.
Political Lesson: Don't give up.

BAD LEGISLATION

Where	Enacted	Law
China	In 2007	Dead Buddhist monks must get permission from the government before being reincarnated.
England	In 1324 (and still in effect)	Sturgeons and whales that wash up on a beach must be given to the country's reigning monarch.
West Bengal, India	In 2006	Cows are required to carry photo ID cards.
Singapore	In 2003	It is illegal to chew gum without a doctor's prescription.
Kentucky, United States	In 1966	It is illegal to sell artificially colored birds or rabbits in quantities of less than six.
England	In 1872	Herding cows while intoxicated is punishable by up to 51 weeks in prison.

Political Brief

The British House of Commons still includes "sword lines"—red lines stitched into the carpet that separate members of opposing parties by two rapier lengths, plus one foot. The boundaries were established in the Middle Ages when legislators still carried swords into the chamber to keep rival members from slashing one another during heated debates.

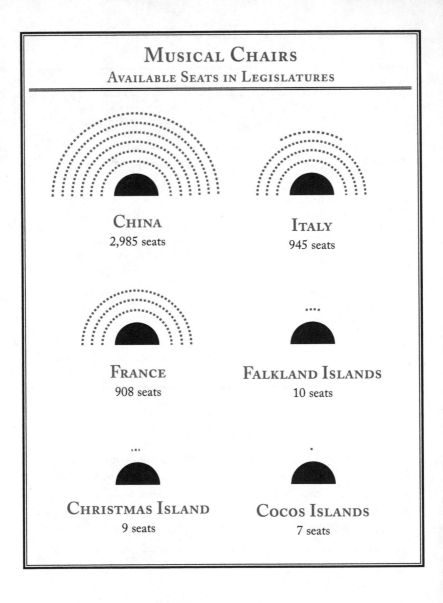

MUSICAL CHAIRS
AVAILABLE SEATS IN LEGISLATURES

CHINA
2,985 seats

ITALY
945 seats

FRANCE
908 seats

FALKLAND ISLANDS
10 seats

CHRISTMAS ISLAND
9 seats

COCOS ISLANDS
7 seats

SENATOR IGNORES NATURE'S CALL, KEEPS TALKING

Determined to maintain the racial status quo in the American South, United States Senator Strom Thurmond decided to take to the United States Senate floor in August of 1957 and keep talking until his colleagues gave up on passing the Civil Rights Act of 1957. The South Carolina senator knew that he would be alone in his filibuster and that if he yielded the floor for even a minute to go to the bathroom, the measure would be voted on and passed. So in the week leading up to the final debate on the bill, Thurmond took lengthy steam baths each day and severely limited his liquid intake. By dehydrating himself beforehand, Thurmond theorized that the water he drank during his filibuster to keep his vocal chords lubricated would go to replenish all the liquid he had sweated out of his body, instead of into his bladder. In case of emergency, Thurmond hid an empty bucket in the cloakroom adjoining the Senate chamber that he could urinate into while still keeping one foot on the Senate floor, technically allowing him to continue holding the floor. The strategy worked for over a day. But instead of voting to table the legislation, Thurmond's fellow senators forced him to just keep talking. Thurmond's own staff finally threw in the towel for him, worried that he would suffer permanent physical damage or even die if he continued. The legislation subsequently passed by an overwhelming majority. But Thurmond still holds the record for the longest solo filibuster in United States Senate history: 24 hours and 18 minutes.

Political Lesson: Sometimes you just have to let go.

LEGISLATION CONSTIPATION

Who	Where and When	To Block
Reverend Fred Nile	Parliament of New South Wales, Australia; 1993	A law making it illegal to vilify gays and lesbians for their sexual orientation
Jean Lassalle	French Parliament; 2003	A measure transferring a police station in his home district
Legislators from the Tamil National Alliance (TNA)	India's Parliament; 2006	A variety of measures that TNA felt discriminated against their constituents
Uri Party legislators	South Korean National Assembly; 2004	The impeachment of President Roh Moo-hyun
Legislators from the Liberal and New Democratic Parties	Canada's Ontario Assembly; 1997	A Conservative Party measure to merge Toronto with several surrounding municipalities
Huey Long of Louisiana	The U.S. Senate; 1935	A bill making changes to the National Recovery Act that would have opened up jobs to Long's enemies in Louisiana

Strategy/How Long	Outcome
Was so eager to get to Parliament to oppose the bill that he fell and broke three ribs; came out of the hospital to filibuster from a wheelchair dressed in his pajamas	The bill passed by a large majority.
Stalled proceedings for several minutes by rising and singing "Majestic Mountains"—a popular anthem in southern France	After Lassalle's singing and his fellow legislators' laughter ended, the measure passed.
Stood shoulder-to-shoulder across the chamber's front entrance, preventing Speaker W.J.M. Lokubandara from entering Parliament to begin the session	The Speaker came in through a side entrance, but was quickly surrounded by the TNA legislators, who shouted slogans and waved signs until Lokubandara canceled the day's session.
Used physical force to seize control of the Speaker's podium and held it for two days, preventing anyone from using it to continue with the assembly's official business	After armed guards dragged the screaming Uri Party lawmakers from the platform, the impeachment vote passed, only to be overturned a few months later in court.
Saddled the bill with over 12,000 amendments, each requiring a separate reading and vote—a process that took ten straight days of nonstop voting, with only one eight-hour break	All of the amendments were voted on and defeated, and the original bill passed.
Took the floor for a filibuster and continued talking for over 15 hours, reading recipes for fried oysters and Roquefort cheese salad dressing when he ran out of things to say about the bill	Long was finally forced to give up the floor so he could urinate and the bill passed while he was in the bathroom.

SPIN CYCLE

HOW TO SURVIVE BEING GRILLED BY A REPORTER

★ Breathe.
When a line of questioning becomes aggressive, oxygenate your blood and brain by taking a deep breath through your nose—not your mouth, which can seem like a gasp. The pause and the increased oxygen will help you formulate a response.

★ Watch your body language.
Avoid the physical signs of lying, such as looking away from, or locking eyes with, the questioner; adjusting clothing; handling objects; or touching your face, nose, mouth, or ears. Avoid defensive gestures such as crossing your arms.

★ Watch your speech.
Avoid verbal signs of lying such as stammering, hesitating, using filler syllables ("uh," "um"), and parroting the questioner's precise language back in your response. Use contractions ("I didn't have sex with that woman"), which are a sign of ease and truth-telling.

★ Praise the question.
Commend the reporter for asking a question that merits an answer.

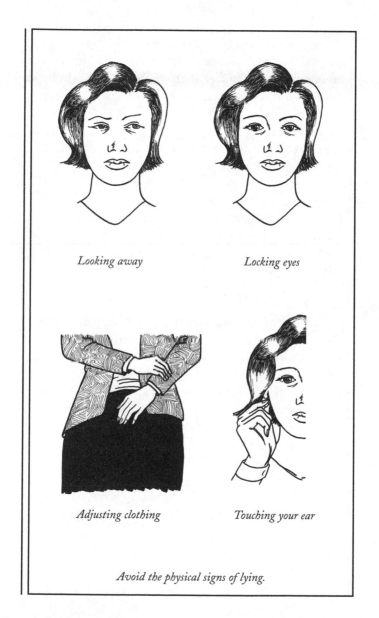

Looking away

Locking eyes

Adjusting clothing

Touching your ear

Avoid the physical signs of lying.

★ **Promise an answer at a later date.**
Suggest that the issue or situation requires further study or investigation, and that it would not be fair to the interest of the voters for you to comment until then.

★ **Restate the obvious.**
Limit your answer to the scope of facts upon which there is already widespread agreement.

★ **Concede minor points.**
By acknowledging inconsequential points, you will build the impression of candor. Then point immediately to achievements that you can claim outweigh any minor missteps.

★ **Keep your cool.**
Do not allow the aggressiveness of the questioning or the emotion of the reporter to influence your response. Maintaining your composure in the face of uncomfortable situations shows that you are able to handle difficult or uncomfortable situations, and that you have nothing to hide.

★ **Question yourself.**
If you do not like the direction of a reporter's questioning, begin to ask yourself questions you would prefer or are prepared to answer by saying, "Are you asking me... ," or "What you're really asking me is...."

LEADING PRESIDENTIAL CANDIDATE CHALLENGES THE PRESS, LOSES

When questioned during an April 1988 *New York Times* interview about rumors he was unfaithful to his wife, the frontrunner for the upcoming United States presidential election Gary Hart responded with a dare. "Follow me around. I don't care. I'm serious. If anybody wants to put a tail on me, go ahead. They'll be very bored." Unbeknownst to Hart, a pair of *Miami Herald* reporters were already tailing him. The week after Hart's "dare" interview, the *Herald* reporters observed a young woman named Donna Rice entering Hart's Washington, D.C., townhouse one evening through its front door. The reporters stayed all night and did not see Rice reemerge. The following morning they confronted Hart as he left the townhouse. Hart claimed Rice was just a friend and had exited the townhouse through its back door shortly after arriving the previous evening. Hart insisted that he had not had sex with Rice or any other woman besides his wife, Lee, since getting married 28 years before. A few days later, the *National Enquirer* published photos of Rice sitting on Hart's lap during a weekend cruise to the Bahamas earlier that year aboard a yacht named *Monkey Business*. Two days later, Hart withdrew from the presidential race.

Political Lesson: Don't go overboard in your denials or invitations.

Journalist-Politician Showdowns

Politician	Journalist
Mamadou Gassama Diaby Member of Parliament (MP) in Mali (1997–2002)	Chahana Takiou, a reporter for *L'Independent*, a biweekly Mali newspaper
John Adams 2nd President of the United States (1797–1801)	Benjamin Franklin Bache, editor of the newspaper *The Philadelphia Aurora*
John Duffy Lead Campaign Strategist for Canada's Liberal Party (2003–)	Canadian Television's Mike Duffy (no relation)
Noel Crichton-Browne Australian Senator (1981–95)	Colleen Egan, reporter from the *Australian*
Jean Bertrand Aristide President of Haiti (1991–96; 2001–04)	Jean Dominique, a popular talk radio host in Haiti
George Bush Sr. and George Bush Jr. 41st and 43rd Presidents of the United States (1989–1993), (2001–09)	CBS TV news anchor Dan Rather

Story	Outcome
Diaby confronted Takiou in the National Assembly chamber over a story Takiou wrote about Diaby bribing a fellow MP, punching and kicking him and then attempting to strangle the journalist, before being pulled off by other MPs.	A nearly unconscious Takiou was rushed to the hospital, while Diaby suffered no legal consequences for his attack.
Newspaper articles criticizing Adams on various issues, including his drafting of the Alien and Sedition Acts of 1798 that made it illegal to criticize Adams in print	Bache was arrested for criticizing Adams in print and died of yellow fever in prison while awaiting trial.
During a 2006 TV interview, Mike Duffy accused John Duffy of trying to intimidate him during a commercial break so that he would not discuss a controversial Liberal Party attack ad.	The controversial Liberal Party ad, which had been quickly pulled due to negative reaction, generated even more negative publicity for Liberals, who were voted out of power three weeks later in the national election.
After Browne showed Egan his secret ballot at a Liberal Party convention, he warned that he would sexually assault her if she reported on what she had seen.	Egan reported the threat and Browne was expelled from the Liberal Party and Senate.
Series of radio commentaries critical of Aristide's government	Dominique was assassinated in 2000 by two gunmen as he pulled into his radio station; suspicions centered on Aristide and his allies, but no one was ever charged.
Questions about Bush Sr.'s role in the Iran-Contra scandal and Bush Jr.'s military service during the Vietnam War	The Bushes both defended themselves vigorously and attacked Rather's journalistic ethics, causing him to back down.

POLITICAL JOURNALIST CHANGES POSITIONS TWICE TOO OFTEN

English journalist Marchamont Needham's writings denouncing the monarchy in his weekly newspaper *Mercurius Britanicus* so angered British King Charles I, the ruler had him jailed in 1646. Charles was in the midst of a civil war against government reformers looking to overthrow him and replace the monarchy with a purely Parliamentarian form of government. While a number of pamphleteers had written critically of Charles' rule, Needham proved particularly vicious and effective. He even published a series of Charles' private letters captured at the Battle of Naseby in 1645, causing the king nearly as much public humiliation as he suffered from losing the battle. After two weeks in prison, Needham underwent a political transformation. He decided he was pro-monarchy and offered his talents to support the king with a new royalist publication *Mercurius Pragmaticus*. Though his metamorphosis won him favor with King Charles, it enraged his former Parliamentarian allies. After they overthrew and executed Charles in 1649, the Parliamentarians tossed Needham in prison. There he underwent a second transformation—renouncing his royalist writings and returning to his Parliamentarian beliefs. Upon his release, Needham began publishing *Mercurius Politicus*, a pro-Parliament newspaper. He continued writing about the virtues of Parliamentarian government and the evils of monarchy until the Parliamentarians were overthrown by monarchists in 1660. When Charles' son, Charles II, reclaimed the throne and reestablished the English monarchy, Needham fled the country.
Political Lesson: Stay the course.

ILL-ADVISED QUOTES

"Don't forget that in the history of the world, there was an election in which Christ and Barabbas were being judged, and the people chose Barabbas."
—*Augusto Pinochet, Chile*

"The truth is that men are tired of liberty."
—*Benito Mussolini, Italy*

"I can be president of the United States, or I can control Alice. I cannot possibly do both."
—*Theodore Roosevelt, United States*, on the behavior of his daughter Alice

"Never believe anything in politics until it has been officially denied."
—*Otto Von Bismarck, Germany*

"All I know about Germany is the toilets in Frankfurt Airport, and that is enough anyway."
—*Jarosław Kaczyński, Poland*

"We are going to take things away from you on behalf of the common good."
—*Hillary Clinton, United States*

"He who does not know how to deceive does not know how to rule."
—*Rafael Trujillo, Dominican Republic*

NEW YORK POLITICAL POWERHOUSE UNDONE BY CARTOONIST

During the mid-19th century, William "Boss" Tweed headed the corrupt Tammany Hall Democratic Party machine that ran New York City. Employing bribery, patronage, intimidation, and violence, Tweed dominated the school system, mayor's office, construction business, and even the courts. To do business with the city, you had to bribe Boss Tweed, who also skimmed a portion of your salary once you gained a job or contract. Though many resented his greed and power, his machine was so wealthy, prevalent, and well-organized, Tweed was regarded as invincible. Tweed's undoing finally came, in large part, due to cartoons. In 1870, when Tweed was at the peak of his influence, editorial cartoonist Thomas Nast began publishing a series of works in *Harper's Weekly* portraying Tweed as an obese, grinning bully lining his pockets at the public's expense and devouring anyone who tried to stop him. Tweed, who suffered little backlash from negative articles about him due to illiterate supporters, grew panicked over the impact of the satirical cartoons. He offered Nast an $8 million bribe to leave the country. Nast declined. Anti-Tweed reform candidates began winning city elections the year after the publication of Nast's first Tweed cartoons. Efforts to prosecute Tweed finally paid off in November 1872 when he was sentenced to 12 years for fraud and corruption. Tweed bribed his way out of prison in 1874 and emigrated to Cuba. Tweed was arrested in Cuba, but escaped and sailed for Spain. U.S. prosecutors found out where Tweed was headed and had Spanish police arrest him when he arrived. The Spanish authorities reportedly used a Thomas Nast cartoon to identify Tweed.

Political Lesson: You can fight City Hall.

HOW TO RESPOND TO BAD PRESS

⭐ Maintain your composure.

No matter how angry you may be, do not allow negative media coverage to prompt you to angry or reckless speech or action. Voters expect their politicians to have thick skins, and the media may delight in pushing the same button if they see that you have reacted in a heated manner.

⭐ Attack the facts.

Have staffers comb the bad press coverage for even minor mistakes or inconsistencies. Use these to cast doubt on the entire substance of the coverage, saying that if the reporters cannot get even the minor facts straight, how could they be trusted with anything more.

⭐ Reframe the situation to stir popular outrage.

Stir up your supporters and potential supporters by framing the attack on you as an attack on them, their families, and their deepest-held values and beliefs, placing yourself on their side. Say, "This is not about me, this is about us." Ask for financial donations and other commitments of support to help you stand up for them against such an "outrage."

Don't dignify it with a response.

★ Pit the media against itself.
Offer to "set the record straight" in special interviews or exclusives to a media outlet that is a rival of the magazine, newspaper, or station that has presented the negative press. The coverage will benefit you at the same time that it gives the media outlet a chance to make its rival look bad or unreliable, and so is likely to be promoted vigorously.

★ Do not respond.
Appear to take the high road by brushing off other reporters' attempts to goad you into comment. Say that you would rather spend your time and energies focusing on the best interests of the voters, and that you wish the media would do the same.

Political Brief

The first professional female journalist in the United States, Anne Royall, was rebuffed in her efforts to gain an interview with the country's president, John Quincy Adams, in 1825. After hearing that Adams started every day with a 5 AM skinny-dip in Washington, D.C.'s Potomac River, Royall ambushed him. When the president emerged from the river naked, he found Royall sitting on his clothes. She refused to let him dress until he conducted an interview with her. Adams agreed and Royall became the first woman to interview a U.S. president.

CHINESE EMPEROR STIFLES HIS CRITICS BY COVERING THEM WITH SIX FEET OF DIRT

The founding father of China, Emperor Qin Shi Hang transformed his homeland from a collection of chaotic, warring states in the 3rd century BC into a unified and powerful nation that remains intact to this day. Qin standardized the country's laws, language, and measurements while establishing an extensive road system. His rule effectively brought an end to centuries of civil war and, with his construction of the Great Wall of China, the threat of invasion from neighboring rivals. But despite his achievements and unprecedented power, Qin still inspired dissent. His harshest critics came from a group of Confucian scholars. They resented the emperor's efforts to standardize Confucian teaching, including his policy of burning texts that did not conform to his narrow, authoritarian interpretation of the philosophy. Qin arrested thousands of his critics and sent them to work on the Great Wall of China, where most workers died of exhaustion within a few weeks. They turned out to be the fortunate ones. Qin ordered 460 of his most vocal critics to come to a spot near his palace where his workers had dug a large ditch. The scholars were herded into the ditch by soldiers, then buried alive.

Political Lesson: Even successful people can overreact to criticism.

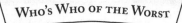

DAN QUAYLE
Vice President of the United States

WORST DEEDS: Unleashing a series of curious, untrue, and bizarre statements during interviews, debates, and speeches, including: "What a waste it is to lose one's mind. Or not to have a mind is being very wasteful. How true that is." ★ "One word sums up probably the responsibility of any governor, and that one word is: 'to be prepared.'" ★ "The Holocaust was an obscene period in our nation's history. I mean in this century's history. But we all lived in this century. I didn't live in this century." ★ "The question is: Are we going to go forward to tomorrow, or past to the back?" ★ "Republicans understand the importance of bondage between a mother and child." ★ "Welcome to President Bush, Mrs. Bush, and my fellow astronauts." ★ "Votes are like trees, if you are trying to build a forest. If you have more trees than you have forests, then at that point the pollsters will probably say you will win." ★ "Verbosity leads to unclear, inarticulate things." ★ "Mars is essentially in the same orbit [as Earth] . . . . Mars is somewhat the same distance from the Sun, which is very important. We have seen pictures where there are canals, we believe, and water. If there is water that means there is oxygen. If oxygen, that means we can breathe." ★ "The American people would not want to know of any misquotes that Dan Quayle may or may not make."

BORN: February 4, 1947 in Indiana

EDUCATION: DePauw University, Indiana University School of Law at Indianapolis

NICKNAME: "Mr. Potatoe Head," in honor of Quayle misspelling "potato" while serving as a judge at a student spelling bee

QUOTE: "I stand by all my misstatements."

THE WRONG SPIN

Politician	Problem	Spin
Maximilien Robespierre Head of the Committee of Public Safety, which ruled France from 1793–94	Justifying his Committee's unleashing of "The Terror," a ten-month period in which the government executed more than 20,000 citizens	"Terror is nothing other than justice, prompt, severe, inflexible; it is therefore an emanation of virtue."
Pravda Official Newspaper of the Soviet Communist Party (1912–91)	Praising another long, dull speech by communist dictator Joseph Stalin in 1935	"Stalin spoke briefly for about an hour."
Marion Barry Mayor of Washington, D.C. (1979–91)(1995–99)	1989 statistics that showed his city had become the murder capital of the United States	"Outside of the killings, we have one of the lowest crime rates in the nation."
Pol Pot Communist Dictator of Cambodia (1975–79)	Explaining why his government killed over two million of its citizens during his reign	"Only several thousand might have died due to some mistakes in implementing our policy of providing an affluent life for the people."
Mobutu Sese Seko President of Zaire (1965–97)	The discovery of Swiss bank accounts in his name	"I would estimate my accounts total less than fifty million dollars. What is that for twenty-two years as head of state in such a big country?"
Jim Gibbons Governor of Nevada (2007–)	Accusation by a waitress that he had fondled her; Gibbons claimed that he had only grabbed the woman after she slipped to prevent her from falling	"Gosh, I learned an important lesson. Never to offer a helping hand to anybody ever again."

CONVICTED POLITICIAN STAGES THE ULTIMATE FAREWELL PRESS CONFERENCE

In 1991, the state treasurer of Pennsylvania, R. Budd Dwyer, was indicted because of a bribery scandal that was centered around a multimillion-dollar accounting contract. Most of the other defendants in the case cut deals with prosecutors and testified against Dwyer, who insisted he was innocent. A jury found Dwyer guilty of receiving a $300,000 kickback bribe. The day before his sentencing hearing, Dwyer called a press conference in the state capital of Harrisburg. He read a prepared statement to reporters, which included television crews filming the event. Dwyer thanked his family and friends for their continued support. He compared his troubles to those faced by the biblical character Job. Dwyer claimed the presiding judge in his case was known for his "medieval sentences" and that he faced a possible 55 years in prison for a crime he still insisted he had not committed. After finishing his prepared statement, Dwyer handed his staffers envelopes containing a suicide note, an organ donor card, and a letter to the governor. He then pulled another envelope from beneath the podium and removed a .357 Magnum handgun from it. He advised those present to "Please leave the room if this will . . . if this will offend you." Dwyer then put the gun in his mouth and pulled the trigger, killing himself instantly. Dwyer's co-defendant in the bribery case, Robert Asher, received a one-year sentence and continued his career in politics after leaving prison. **Political Lesson:** Don't do it.

HOW TO ANONYMOUSLY LEAK INFORMATION TO THE MEDIA

⭐ Go "off the record."
Speak to a reporter you trust "off the record" as a "background source." This accepted but unofficial arrangement means that while you are passing along information, the reporter cannot cite you as an official source, and must confirm the information elsewhere before using it in a story. Provide the reporter with a list of people or other sources of information, such as court documents, where the tip can be validated.

⭐ Use the blogosphere.
Through a third party, pass the information to a blogger with a large or influential audience, and wait. Once the information is repeated and spread on other blogs and chat boards, print and on-air journalists will either report it, or report on the fact that others are reporting it. The effect of introducing the leaked information will be the same.

⭐ Spread it as gossip.
Because they are professionally attuned to seeking out information, journalists are often eager gossips. Find out what bars, coffee shops, health clubs, or other public places that useful journalists hang out in; give the

Go "deep throat" and pass along information to a reporter.

information that you want leaked to a staffer or some-one who also frequents those places to pass along.

⭐ Start at the bottom.
Instruct one of your lower-level staffers or volunteers to pass along the information to an ambitious intern or hungry, entry-level reporter at a key news source, then watch the information work its way up the ladder and into print or on air.

⭐ Play ding-dong-ditch.
Put the information in an envelope with a reporter's name on it and have it mailed anonymously, or slip it under her door when no one is around.

⭐ Go "deep throat."
Instruct a trusted aide to become a consistent, secret source of information for a powerful journalist who will repay your favors by using the information you pass along against your enemies.

Political Brief

During the campaign for the United States presidency in 1800, members of the Federalist Party anonymously placed stories in several leading newspapers that the Democratic-Republican Party nominee Thomas Jefferson had died.

AUSTRALIAN POLITICIAN JAILED OVER PHONE THREATS

On June 16, 1993, a man disguising his voice with a fake Italian accent and claiming to be a mafia hitman called the local newspaper in the town of Blue Mountain in New South Wales, Australia. He threatened to blow up John Pascoe, an environmental activist and member of the town's city council. In previous weeks, Pascoe had received menacing telephone calls from a man disguising his voice with a fake Chinese accent. Local authorities took the strange threats seriously. After tracing the threatening phone calls, police concluded they had been placed by former Blue Mountain mayor Barry Morris. As the owner of a local oil company and a pro-development mayor, Barry Morris often butted heads with members of the Blue Mountain city council during the 1980s. Morris and his Liberal Party wanted to transform the small, rural community into a booming tourist destination and business center, while his Labor Party rivals sought to preserve the area's relatively pristine natural state and unique character. Morris left the mayor's office and was elected as Blue Mountain's representative to the Australian Parliament in 1988. But he remained bitter over his clashes with his hometown's city council members. In late 1995, Morris was convicted of making the threatening phone calls and sentenced to two years in prison.

Political Lesson: Play fair and don't be a sore loser.

SNUBBING PHILIPPINES FIRST LADY NEARLY COSTS THE BEATLES THEIR LIVES

On July 3, 1966, the enormously popular British rock band the Beatles arrived in the Philippines for two concerts. First Lady Imelda Marcos invited the band to a brunch at the presidential palace. But exhausted and worried about making their first show on time, the band declined. A national beauty pageant winner and the wife of the most powerful man in the country, Imelda Marcos expected people to show up when she summoned them. The Beatles' snub was particularly embarrassing to her. She had invited more than 300 children from influential families to the brunch. Marcos also brought in TV camera crews. She wanted them to see her hosting—and perhaps even singing with—the most popular band in the world. But they ended up only with footage of crying, disappointed children. The next morning, the Beatles awoke to find out that they had received death threats and their Filipino security crew had mysteriously disappeared, along with their cars and drivers. Concerned about their safety, the band and their aides rushed to the airport to fly out of the country. But an angry mob was waiting for them on the runway. The band and their entourage were pushed, punched, knocked down, spit on, and screamed at by hundreds of Marcos supporters. After making it onto the plane, the band's manager Brian Epstein was forced to get off and turn over all the money the band had made from the two sold-out concerts the previous night before they could take off. The Philippines incident played a large part in the Beatles deciding to never tour again after 1966. Twenty years later when Imelda Marcos and her husband Ferdinand were forced to flee the Philippines themselves, authorities searching their presidential palace discovered, among many other things, aborted plans to assassinate the Beatles to avenge their snubbing of Imelda's brunch invitation.

Political Lesson: Understand the importance of protocol when visiting foreign countries.

Lyric vs. Rhetoric
Musician-Politician Feuds

Who	Conflict	Climax
Ludwig van Beethoven vs. Napoleon Bonaparte (1804–1814, 1815)	Beethoven denounced Napoleon after Napoleon crowned himself Emperor of France in 1804.	Beethoven changed the name of his Third Symphony from the "Bonaparte Symphony" to "Heroic" and dedicated it to "the memory of a great man."
British musician and former Beatle John Lennon vs. U.S. President Richard Nixon (1969–74)	In 1972, Lennon planned a nationwide tour to energize young voters to support candidates opposed to the Vietnam War, which Nixon had escalated.	The Nixon administration moved to have Lennon deported from the United States.
Fela Kuti, Nigerian Musician and Political Activist vs. Yakubu Gowon, Military Dictator of Nigeria (1966–75)	A socialist, Kuti became increasingly critical of Gowon's dictatorship in his songs and set up a Nigerian commune, which he declared independent of Gowon's rule.	In 1974, Gowon's men raided the commune and planted pot on Kuti, who ate the joint to prevent its use as evidence.
Jamaican reggae artist Bob Marley vs. Edward Seaga, Head of Jamaica's Labour Party (1974–2005)	In 1976, Marley agreed to play Smile Jamaica, a free concert organized by socialist Prime Minister Michael Manley, angering Manley's right-wing rival Seaga.	Three days before the concert, gunmen thought to be connected to Seaga broke into Marley's compound and shot him, his wife, and manager.
Peter Garrett of the Australian rock band Midnight Oil vs. Australian Prime Minister John Howard (1996–)	Garrett, a left-wing activist, often criticized the conservative Howard, especially for his refusal to apologize for the Australian government's mistreatment of Aborigines.	Garrett took it upon himself to apologize at the closing ceremonies of the 2000 Summer Olympics in Sydney, when he and his bandmates performed in black sweatsuits with the word "Sorry" printed on them.

HOW TO SIMPLIFY A COMPLICATED MESSAGE

⭐ Be emotional.
Effective and memorable political messages depend on inspiring emotional responses from voters that drive them to polls. Invigorate your material with emotion suggestive of deep engagement in the issue or situation. Most voters vote with their hearts first.

⭐ Draw a picture.
Reduce the issue or situation to a single image or pair of opposing images in which it is clear what is good and what is bad. A criminal walking through a revolving prison door, or a child holding a flower pointed at a soldier with a rifle are strong images. The direct connection between the images and the issue are less important than the positive or negative emotional reactions that they stir in support of your campaign or against your opponent's campaign.

⭐ Use an analogy.
In circumstances where visuals cannot be readily used, describe the situation or issue in terms of a familiar, folksy saying in which it is obvious what is preferable, in a way that even the least sophisticated of voters can understand and appreciate. Associate your opponent with the negative aspect or outcome.

Reduce the issue to a pair of opposing images in which it is clear what is good and what is bad.

Remove all doubt.
Remove all shading, nuance, or equivocation from your statements about the issue. State that any acknowledgment of complication surrounding the issue by your opponent is a sign of weakness or being "soft" on the matter at hand.

 Compare and contrast.
Paint the issue as a conflict in the broadest possible terms, between right and wrong, or good and evil. Point out that your side is right and good, while the opposition is wrong and evil.

Be Aware
If simplifying a complicated message or stance does not sufficiently boost your stature with voters, shift attention to another issue upon which a firm position may yield clearer results, or prove to be a more significant or complicated liability for your opponent.

Political Brief

During a 1976 campaign appearance in Binghamton, New York, United States Vice President Nelson Rockefeller responded to protesters by giving them the middle finger. The gesture, which Rockefeller performed with a toothy grin, was captured by photographers and printed in newspapers across the world the following day.

PROTESTERS GET BIGGEST PIECE OF MEDIA PIE

Organizers of a July 1982 Washington, D.C., event thought they had found the perfect way to celebrate the recent passage of President Ronald Reagan's tax cut legislation. The conservative United States Senate Republican Conference created the "world's largest apple pie" and invited everyone to come to the Capitol Mall to get a piece as a symbolic way of showing the tax cuts' alleged universal benefits. Members of the Community for Creative Nonviolence (CCNV), a progressive political activist group that also runs a homeless shelter in Washington, D.C., disagreed with the tax cuts. They believed that Reagan's fiscal policies only benefited the rich and punished the poor by paying for the tax cuts through reductions in social programs. To get their point across, five CCNV members arrived at the apple pie ceremony dressed in top hats and oversized tuxedoes stuffed with pillows to make them look obese. They hung signs around their necks identifying themselves as "Bankers," "CEOs," "Fat Cats," "Corporations," and "Lobbyists." As event organizers got ready to distribute pieces of the pie, five CCNV protesters rushed through the crowd and belly-flopped into the pie, shouting "IT'S ALL MINE! IT'S ALL MINE!" The protesters rolled around, shoveling handfuls of pie into their faces and pretending to try to eat it all themselves. By the time police arrived, the pie and the event had been ruined.

Political Lesson: Don't let someone else hijack your media event.

WORST CAMPAIGN SLOGANS

Joke! Joke! Joke-ker!

Race: 2000 Philippines
National Senate
Candidate: Joker Arroyo

We need Adlai Badly

Race: 1952 U.S. President
Candidate: Adlai Stevenson

Perón or DEAD

Race: 1946 Argentine President
Candidate: Juan Perón

Don't Waste Your Vote, Give It To Me

Race: 2006 Governor of
New York
Candidate: Malachy McCourt

In Your Heart, You Know He's RIGHT

Race: 1964 U.S. President
Candidate: Barry Goldwater

Keep the Bastards Honest

Race: 1980 Australian
National Elections
Candidate: Don Chipp

An Almond in Every Pot

Race: 1946 Mayor of
Cuhr, Switzerland
Candidate: Bruno Farber

Rumsey-Rumsey, Dumpsey-Dumpsey, Colonel Johnson Killed Tecumseh

Race: 1836 U.S. President
Candidate: Col. Richard
Mentor Johnson
(Running Mate to
Martin Van Buren)

INDONESIAN PRESIDENT DOZES OFF DURING CRITICAL SPEECH

By the middle of 2000, Indonesian President Abdurrahman Wahid found himself in deep political trouble. The nation's economy was reeling on the brink of collapse. Several members of Wahid's inner circle were embroiled in serious corruption scandals. Civil war raged on several fronts and many of his own Cabinet ministers were openly calling for his removal from office. Wahid believed he could revive his credibility and presidency with an August speech before the Indonesian People's Assembly, the national body that had elected him the previous autumn. Wahid's address sought to apologize and offer solutions for the problems the government faced, while inspiring new confidence in his ability to implement those remedies. Wahid nodded off to sleep several times during his own 90-minute address, however. At one point, he warned that ongoing religious wars between the nation's Muslims and Christians threatened to tear the country apart, then dozed off again. The following year, the Assembly voted unanimously to impeach him.

Political Lesson: Do not fall asleep during your own speech.

Political Brief

As a young man, Greek politician Demosthenes (384–322 BC) thwarted the temptation to skip practicing rhetoric by shaving half his head and beard so he wouldn't go out and socialize. Temporarily disfigured, Demosthenes remained inside for weeks studying the works of great orators and practicing his own speeches until his hair grew back. Demosthenes went on to use his rhetorical skills to become the leading political figure in Athens and compel the city into a disastrous war with Phillip of Macedon and his son Alexander the Great.

HOW TO GIVE YOURSELF A POLITICAL MAKEOVER

1 Audit your appearance.

Take a long, hard look at yourself. Ask trusted colleagues and family members to evaluate how you look and take notes on your strengths and weaknesses. Your physical appearance delivers the first and most lasting impression of you as a person and politician to voters. If voters are not responding to your message, it may be because your appearance is either distracting from or working against the impression you wish to give. Your hair, wardrobe, facial expressions, and body language are all interpreted as measures of your abilities and aptitude.

2 Neutralize negative features.

Do not seek to turn every aspect of your appearance into a shining asset or you will risk overcompensating in a way that can draw still more attention to your flaws. Seek to deflect attention from what is a given (height, weight, ugliness) and change what you can.

3 Establish a core look.

Select signature clothing styles, personal details, or physical mannerisms that will form the foundation of the new political identity you wish to convey.

Translate your desired impression into a fashion statement: decisive leadership (loud, colored accessories), steadfast and reliable (a sober hairstyle), someone who gets things done (shirtsleeves rolled up or hair pulled back), or the friendliest candidate (calculatedly unpolished.)

4 Accessorize.
Use different fashion accessories to adjust your core look to the variety of events and locations you encounter. A hat, a clipboard, or a hot dog can complement, not compete, with your basic look.

5 Avoid trends.
Resist the temptation to adopt trendy fashions and hairstyles, which may make you momentarily popular with younger voters, but risk giving the impression that you spend too much time refining your appearance rather than considering substantive issues, or tagging your candidacy to a fashion look that may not last very long or suit you very well.

6 Blunt your sexiness.
While being attractive is an advantage in politics, being sexy can seem threatening. Voters want candidates who are easy on the eyes, but not hot.

Blunt your sexiness.

7 | Mirror success.

If you are unsure what look to adopt, consider the style and appearance details of successful candidates with whom you are not directly competing and copy his or her look.

Political Brief

A tailor by trade, United States President Andrew Johnson (1865–69) hand-made clothing for all of his Cabinet ministers and insisted that they wear them on official occasions.

POLITICAL FASHION STATEMENTS

Who	Fashion Statement	Symbolized
Mobutu Sese Seko President of Zaire 1965–97	Leopardskin Toque	That even in a modern "democracy" he still wields the same authority of a traditional tribal chief
Michael Foot Leader British House of Commons 1976–79	Donkey Jacket	The Labor Party leader's continuing connection to the working class
George IV King of England 1820–30	Modern men's suit with necktie	Transition to more functional style of dress and business-oriented government
Jawaharlal Nehru Prime Minister of India 1947–64	The Nehru Jacket	Increased integration of Asian and Western cultures
Marie Antoinette Queen of France 1774–92	"Pouf" Hairdo whose width and height asserted social superiority	Power and prestige, with the extra volume of hair providing space for symbolic ornamentation with ribbons and jewels
Julius Caesar Roman Dictator 49–44 BC	Robe of "Imperial" purple	Absolute power, which could only be wielded by the head of state
Mike Defensor Presidential Chief of Staff of Philippines 2006–07	Pink Dental Braces	Ability to cheerfully take on difficult issues and turn them into positives

CHURCH LEADER AND POLITICIAN GOES TOO FAR, DICTATES FASHION

A member of the fledgling Mormon Church in Illinois, James Jesse Strang declared himself as the church's new leader after its founder Joseph Smith was murdered in 1844. While most of Smith's flock followed Brigham Young to Utah, Smith led 300 converts to an island on northern Lake Michigan, which he renamed Zion. Strang was coronated as King James I of Zion in a ceremony led by his prime minister, George Adams, a former Shakespearean actor. Recognizing the importance of good visual props for the ceremony, Adams lent Strang a metal crown, scepter, and a flannel robe that he had once worn on stage while playing Macbeth. When word of Strang's "kingdom" reached Washington, D.C., President Millard Fillmore ordered his arrest on charges of treason. Swayed by his eloquence and claims of religious persecution, a federal jury in Detroit acquitted Strang in 1853. Publicity from the trial helped Strang win a seat later that year in the Michigan state legislature, where he rebuffed early attempts to oust him and went on to pass five bills in his first session. Back on Zion, King James instituted numerous measures to promote racial and gender equality, plus the establishment of pensions for the elderly and the setting aside of wilderness areas. Strang also ordered all his female subjects to wear miniskirts and pantaloons, or "bloomers," angering many of his subjects. Two men whose wives were particularly outraged by Strang's fashion edict attacked Strang on a dock on June 16, 1856. They shot Strang twice in the back, then punched and kicked him as he lay dying. When they saw what was happening to their king, many of Strang's subjects joined in the beating.

Political Lesson: Separate church, state, and fashion.

CHAPTER 4
SCANDALS AND CORRUPTION

NO COMMENT

THE ULTIMATE COVER-UP ARTIST

Like most politicians, T.J. Ley gained his share of enemies during his career. But few politicians managed to lose so many enemies under mysterious circumstances as the conservative Australian. During his first campaign for the Australian House of Representatives, Ley's Labor Party opponent, Fred McDonald, presented evidence that Ley had attempted to bribe him out of the race. McDonald lodged a legal complaint, but disappeared before the case came to trial. He was never seen again. The following year, Hymann Goldstein, a partner with Ley in a new herbicide business, complained that Ley had spent all of their investors' money vacationing with his mistress. Goldstein was found dead a short time later at the bottom of a cliff. When Keith Greendor was hired to investigate Goldstein's death, he fell off a boat and drowned. Questions about the growing number of bodies in Ley's wake helped lead to his losing his bid for reelection in 1928. He relocated to England with his mistress Maggie Brooke, leaving his wife behind in Australia. During World War II, Ley was convicted of black marketeering. Around the same time, Ley began to suspect his mistress Brooke of carrying on an affair with John McMain. In 1946, McMain's body was found in a chalk-pit, strangled and severely beaten. Ley was convicted of McMain's murder, but escaped the death sentence by pleading insanity. He died in an English asylum in 1947, insisting to the end that he was innocent of all the murders and mysterious disappearances that had befallen his enemies.

Political Lesson: Don't try to bury real skeletons.

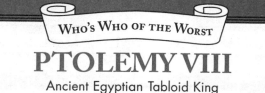

PTOLEMY VIII

Ancient Egyptian Tabloid King

WORST DEEDS: Marrying his sister Cleopatra II, then killing her young son as she held him in her arms at their wedding reception to clear up any doubts about his claims to becoming the next pharaoh ★ Marrying his new wife Cleopatra II's daughter while still married to Cleopatra II ★ Disgusting his citizens so thoroughly that they set fire to his palace in 132 BC, forcing him to flee to Cyprus ★ Kidnapping and killing his own 12-year-old son Memphistes, then dismembering him, packing the pieces in a box, and sending them to his mother Cleopatra II back in Egypt as revenge for her having Memphistes declared pharaoh while he hid in Cyprus ★ Returning to power in Egypt, but sapping the country's military and economic resources through decades of civil war, power struggles, further scandal, and incompetent governance, forcing the Romans to come in after his death to try to revive the country ★ Trying to get his elephants to trample a crowd of Jews in Alexandria who disputed his claim to the throne, only to have the elephants turn and charge him and his men

BORN: 182 BC

DIED: June 26, 116 BC

PHYSICAL APPEARANCE: A "monstrous" face with a short and extremely obese body that he liked to show off by wearing see-through gauze clothing in public

NICKNAME: Though he ordered his subjects to call him Euergetes (which roughly translates as "The Benevolent One"), most of them referred to him as Physcon (which roughly translates as "Potbelly")

QUOTE: "Through indulgence in luxury, his body had become corrupted with fat and with a belly of such size that it would have been hard to measure it with one's arms." —Athenaeus, ancient Egyptian historian

Name	Where	Scandal
The Dreyfus Affair	France (the 1890s)	Alfred Dreyfus, a Jewish officer in the French army, was wrongly convicted of treason and imprisoned on Devil's Island.
The Cuban Pouches Scandal	Chile (1972)	Cuba was secretly sending arms to Chile's socialist president, Salvador Allende, inside of diplomatic pouches so they could not be inspected by customs officials.
Watergate	United States (1972–74)	Men hired to perform dirty tricks by the Republican Party broke in to the Democratic Party's campaign headquarters in Washington, D.C., in 1972 to set up wiretaps, but were caught by police.
Iraq-Gate	Finland (2003)	Post-election revelations emerged that Finnish Prime Minister Anneli Jaatteenmaki had used information from secret government documents during her successful campaign to unseat Prime Minister Paavo Lipponen.
SARS Outbreak	China (2003)	In February 2003, the Chinese government began receiving reports of a deadly outbreak of SARS (Sudden Acute Respiratory Syndrome), including cases in the capital, Bejiing.
The Mark Foley Page Scandal	United States (2006)	Emergence of sexually explicit e-mails sent by Republican Congressman Mark Foley to several teenaged boys who served as Congressional pages.

THE SCANDAL THEY TRIED TO COVER UP

Cover-up	Outcome
The French government suppressed evidence of anti-Semitic motivations behind Dreyfus's prosecution and procedural misdeeds, which were later exposed by famed French writer Émile Zola and others.	Reports of the cover-up caused the country to split into pro-Dreyfus and anti-Dreyfus factions—deep divisions that remained even after Dreyfus's 1899 pardon.
After reports of a particularly large shipment emerged, Allende offered conflicting explanations, claiming the packages contained everything from cigarettes to paintings for a Cuban art exhibit.	Allende's waffling increased doubts about his integrity and his relationship with the communist Castro, helping embolden right-wing army officers led by Augusto Pinochet to overthrow him the following year.
President Richard Nixon instructed his aides to stall the investigation and conceal his reelection campaign's connection to the crime.	The web of connections slowly unraveled, leading to hearings in Congress in 1974 calling for Nixon's impeachment for obstruction of justice, followed by Nixon's resignation.
Instead of coming clean, Jaatteenmaki denied that she knew the source of the information, saying someone anonymous had faxed the documents to her without her asking.	When irrefutable evidence emerged that Jaatteenmaki had requested the documents and was lying, she was forced to resign after only one month in office.
Bejiing mayor Meng Xuenong and national health minister Zhang Wenkang allegedly ordered SARS patients shuffled between hospitals to keep people from realizing that a serious outbreak was occurring.	Moving the SARS patients around helped spread the disease, leading to more deaths and to the firing of Xuenong and Wenkang, though many regard them as scapegoats for a wider government cover-up.
Republican leaders in Congress failed to discipline Foley after learning of his behavior.	Emerging in the media less than six weeks before the 2006 elections, the scandal and cover-up helped lead to the Democratic takeover of Congress.

BINGO-GATE ROCKS CANADIAN POLITICAL WORLD

To pad their budget in the 1990s, British Columbia's ruling New Democratic Party (NDP) ran crooked bingo games. While proceeds were supposed to all go to local charities, over $2.5 million actually got skimmed off the top of bingo entry fees and rerouted through the Nainamo Commonwealth Holding Society into NDP coffers. British Columbia Premier and NDP chief Michael Harcourt stepped down over the scandal. Though not directly involved in Bingo-gate, Harcourt said, as Party leader, he needed to take responsibility for the fiasco. NDP cabinet minister Dave Stupich resigned after confessing to masterminding the scheme. Due to his failing health and onset of dementia, the 77-year-old received only a two-year sentence of house arrest in 1999. Investigators continued to look into the scheme, but abandoned their Bingo-gate inquiry in 2001 because the web of financial transactions weaved by Stupich, a former accountant, proved too complex to unravel.

Political Lesson: You can be implicated, even if you're not involved.

Political Brief

Concerned that his Secretary of State's habit of cavorting in public with beautiful young women would lead to a sex scandal, United States President Richard Nixon ordered Henry Kissinger in 1970 to start bringing older, less attractive women as dates to White House social functions.

CHINA'S CULTURAL REVOLUTION

Government Program

WORST DEEDS: Unleashing the "Red Guards," a cultural army made up of hundreds of thousands of youths and workers to reeducate the Chinese population in Marxist-Maoist thinking while eliminating cultural and intellectual "relics" of the past ★ Destroying countless precious artworks, antiques, books, and historical sites ★ Leading ideological purges of the Chinese Communist Party, the government, citizens, and competing factions of the Guard itself, calling millions out as class enemies and subject to public humiliation, forced labor, and execution ★ Throwing the country into a state of chaos, stalling its economy and derailing its educational system in service of internal political struggles played out across the general population ★ Insinuating Mao Tse Tung's cult of personality into every level of Chinese society ★ Covering for the failures of the Communist Party's disastrous Great Leap Forward collectivizing program, which resulted in widespread famines and the deaths of as many as 30 million people

CREATED: May 16, 1966

ENDED: October 6, 1976

NICKNAME: The Great Proletarian Cultural Revolution

QUOTE: "Revolution is not a dinner party, not an essay, nor a painting, nor a piece of embroidery; it cannot be advanced softly, gradually, carefully, considerately, respectfully, politely, plainly, and modestly." —Mao Tse Tung

HOW TO SURVIVE A SEX SCANDAL

1   Circle the family.
Gather your spouse, children, and any other available family members for a photo-op showing them standing around you looking proud and trusting. Invite the press to film you at a family picnic or volleyball game. Present yourself as a solid family person whose family members continue to support you.

2   Respond quickly.
If the allegations of sexual impropriety are true and can be proven, apologize and say you have asked your family for forgiveness and they have granted it. Then ask voters for forgiveness. If charges against you are false—or true but cannot be proven—vigorously deny them in front of media cameras and urge reporters to respect you and your family's privacy.

3   Do not lie.
Providing inaccurate accounts of your activities may create a whole new avenue for problems.

4   Move on.
When pressed about the scandal by reporters, say you want to focus on issues that affect the everyday lives of your constituents rather than your personal life. Invite the press along to film you engaging in job-related activities such as talking to voters or signing legislation.

Only appear in wholesome family situations.

Present yourself as someone who is too dedicated to his work to let a personal crisis keep him from going forward with more important matters.

5 Leave town.
If the scandal persists, arrange travel on official business. Do not allow reporters to go along and do not give a press conference when you arrive. Be visible and untroubled, but not quotable. If you cut off reporters' access to you, the story may die down.

6 Take refuge in rehab.
If the furor over the scandal does not dissipate, declare that you have an alcohol or prescription drug dependency that drove you to the impropriety. Then check into a secure and secluded rehabilitation clinic.

7 Ask for forgiveness.
Upon checking out of the rehab clinic, declare that you are cured and now a far better person who can't wait to get back to working for voters. Ask again for forgiveness and vow to work even harder on important issues.

8 Declare war.
If scandal refuses to die down, announce a bold new initiative such as a war against crime, or if you are in position to do so, declare war on a small country.

Be Aware
Outside of England and the United States, sexual dalliances are more casually considered by the public.

ROYAL WARLORD DETHRONED AFTER MARRYING MOVIE STAR

A cross-dressing princess, military leader, and ingenious entrepreneur, Olive Yang was born in 1927, the eldest daughter of the royal family of the Shan, an expatriate Chinese clan that dominates large parts of Burma. Known as "Miss Hairy Legs" to her fellow students, Yang used the pistol she carried in her school bag, her royal stature, and her bullying nature to terrify the other children into submission. As a teenager, Yang harnessed her entrepreneurial genius to take over the drug trade in Asia's Golden Triangle, which had become the center of world opium production after World War II. Wearing a gray military uniform she designed and a Belgian pistol on each hip, Yang organized her own army, and by the age of 19 commanded over a thousand soldiers known as Olive's Boys. She strong-armed highland opium growers into increasing harvests and took control of moving the drugs down to the lowlands. Yang employed her political connections and growing relationship with the CIA to transport the opium across the border into Thailand. The huge profits she enjoyed from her operation allowed Yang to increase her military strength and political power. It also emboldened her to begin living openly as a lesbian. Though Yang's royal family had looked the other way during her years of brutality and drug-running, her new unabashed sexuality finally compelled them to take action. When Olive Yang announced she had married her girlfriend—Burma's leading film actress Wa Wa Win Shwe—her brother had her arrested and put into an asylum. Stripped of her military might, financial resources, and aura of invincibility, Olive Yang emerged several years later and decided to live the rest of her life as a nun.

Political Lesson: Know your limitations.

Sex Scandals

Politician	Partner	Scandal
Domitian Roman Emperor AD 81–96	Vestal Virgins	Domitian, no stranger to perversion himself, accused the Vestal Virgins of immoral sexual behavior.
Arthur Brown U.S. Senator from Utah 1896–97	Anna Maddison Bradley	The married Brown carried on a long-running affair with Bradley.
Margaret Trudeau First Lady of Canada 1971–77	Linked to numerous men, including U.S. Senator Ted Kennedy and Rolling Stones' guitarist Ron Wood	Margaret became a high-profile tabloid regular in the mid-'70s, often pictured at hot night spots partying with other men.
James Buchanan U.S. President 1857–1861	William Rufus King	Buchanan, a lifelong bachelor, lived for 15 years with his "close friend" William Rufus King, a senator from Alabama.
Charles Stewart Parnell Leader of the Irish Parliamentary Party and "Uncrowned King of Ireland" during the late 19th century	Kitty O'Shea	Parnell engaged in a longtime affair with O'Shea, who was married to another man.
Chu Mei-feng Taipei City Councilperson 1994–98	Unnamed married businessman	A secret surveillance tape from Chu's apartment released to the media showed a tryst between a married businessman and Chu.

UNITED STATES PRESIDENT ADMITS SEXUAL AFFAIR, WINS ELECTION

When reports emerged early in the 1884 American presidential campaign that Democratic nominee Grover Cleveland had fathered an illegitimate child the previous decade, Republicans felt confident that they would win the White House in a landslide. They even began to taunt Cleveland at their campaign rallies with the chant, "Ma, Ma. Where's My Pa? Gone to the White House, ha, ha, ha!" Instead of trying to deny the rumor, Cleveland told the truth. While working as a lawyer early in his career, Cleveland had engaged in a brief affair with the boy's mother, Maria Halpin, around the time her son was conceived. Halpin was also engaged in a number of other affairs during the same period, including one with Cleveland's law partner. Cleveland never believed he was the boy's father. But since all her other lovers were married and unlikely to come forward, Cleveland had agreed to become the boy's legal father and pay for his upbringing and education. When the full story came out, Cleveland's popularity actually increased. He beat Republican nominee James G. Blaine handily in November to win the White House. **Political Lesson:** You never know how the public will react.

Political Brief

During an official state dinner during a diplomatic mission to Japan in 1992, U.S. President George H.W. Bush vomited on the pants of Japanese Prime Minister Kiichi Miyazawa, then passed out on Miyazawa's lap. Bush attributed his nausea to the stomach flu.

POLITICAL ASYLUM
U.S. POLITICIANS WHO ENTERED REHAB DURING SCANDALS

Politician	Problem	Solution
Jon C. Hinson U.S. Representative from Mississippi (1979–81)	Was arrested in 1976 for exposing himself to solicit sex from an undercover police officer in Arlington National Cemetery	Claimed he wasn't exposing himself for sex, but because he was drunk, then checked into an alcohol rehabilitation center
Bob Baumann U.S. Representative from Maryland (1973–81)	A leading family values advocate, Baumann was caught having sex with a 16-year-old boy in the back of his car on a Washington, D.C., street	Blamed the incident on his "acute alcoholism" and checked into rehab
Bob Packwood U.S. Senator from Oregon (1968–95)	In 1994, ten women who had worked or lobbied for Packwood during his time in the Senate accused him of sexual abuse	Apologized, blamed his tough childhood and alcoholism for his sexual improprieties, and checked into an alcohol rehabilitation center
Bob Ney U.S. Representative from Ohio (1995–2006)	Indicted for perjury and trading legislative favors for gifts with infamous lobbyist Jack Abramoff in 2006	Confessed to his crimes but blamed alcoholism and entered a private substance abuse clinic
Patrick Kennedy U.S. Representative from Rhode Island (1995–)	Late-night car crash into a barricade in Washington, D.C., in March 2006	Claimed the crash had resulted from his addiction to prescription painkillers and entered the drug rehab wing of the Mayo Clinic in Minnesota
Thomas Ravenal South Carolina Treasurer (2006–07)	Indicted in June 2007 on federal cocaine distribution charges	Claimed he just bought the coke to share with friends and spent a month each in rehab centers in New Mexico and Arizona to work on "reckless behavior" issues left over from his childhood

POWERFUL CONGRESSMAN LOSES CAREER BUT PIONEERS NEW SCANDAL SURVIVAL STRATEGY

Just after midnight on October 7, 1974, United States Park Police in Washington, D.C., pulled over the car of veteran congressman Wilbur Mills because his driver had failed to turn on the headlights. Mills was sitting in the backseat with Fanne Foxe, an exotic dancer who went by the stage name "The Argentine Firecracker." Both were drunk, with Mills bleeding from a recent blow delivered by Foxe. When police approached the car, Foxe fled and dove into the Tidal Basin, a shallow inlet adjoining the Potomac River, and tried to swim away. As Chairman of the House Ways and Means Committee, Mills controlled the allocation of nearly every dollar spent by the United States government. Many regarded the 17-term congressman as the most powerful and respected person in Washington, D.C. Though publicly humiliated by the drunken incident with Foxe, Mills easily won reelection a few weeks later. The following month, Mills traveled to Boston to see Foxe, who was now performing as "The Tidal Basin Bombshell." Mills joined Foxe onstage at the Pilgrim Theater, a burlesque club in the city's red-light district. Foxe introduced "Mr. Mills" to her audience and kissed him on the cheek. Mills blamed his strange behavior on alcoholism and checked into a rehabilitation center in Florida. But when he emerged the following month, his congressional colleagues insisted he step down as Chairman of the Ways and Means Committee. Although he would continue to serve as congressman for another two years, Mills later decided not to seek another term. During his retirement, he helped raise money for substance abuse treatment centers and saw such centers become a favorite refuge for United States politicians trying to ride out scandals.

Political Lesson: Pioneers usually don't fare as well as those who follow in their footsteps.

HOW TO MANIPULATE AN ANGRY MOB

1 Position yourself above the crowd.
Find a spot overlooking the main body of the mob where they can all see you—and hear you. Use a bull-horn or microphone if the crowd is too large to hear you shouting.

2 Do not be intimidated.
The mob can most likely tear you apart if it wants to, so getting upset won't do any good. Stay calm.

3 Think of the mob as a single organism.
Formulate your response as if you were dealing with one very angry person. Determine what caused that person to become irate.

4 Get the mob's attention.
Do or say something dramatic to get everyone looking at you—and waiting to see or hear what you will do next. Smash a statue with a sledgehammer or fire a pistol. Your gesture should not be so dramatic that it frightens the mob and causes them to rampage or attack you.

5 Stroke the mob's ego.
Praise the mob for forming. Tie their formation to the desire to defend a traditional value still shared by most people. Get them thinking as one so you can get them to act as one.

Invoke symbols of unity, such as the national soccer team.

6 Use popular symbolism.

Employ a visual aid, like a flag, that easily symbolizes a traditional value. Use another object to represent the threat. Hold the flag aloft and praise the values it represents, then hold a burning torch near it, identifying the torch as the main threat to the imperiled traditional value. If no physical objects are available, invoke other symbols of unity, such as the national soccer team.

7 Point to your opponents as the problem.

Identify the crisis that caused the mob to gather, then identify your main political rivals as the ones causing the crisis. Accuse them of bringing on the crisis through their flagrant disregard of the traditional value you invoked earlier. Get the mob members thinking of your enemies as their enemies.

8 Offer a solution.

Funnel the mob's anger and energy toward a single action against your political rivals and for the defense of the imperiled traditional value. Tell the crowd to vote out the scoundrels who caused the crisis, or, if no election is imminent, to hold an even bigger demonstration next week.

9 Employ a catchphrase.

Simplify the main theme of your rhetoric into a simple catchphrase—"The future belongs to us" or "All you need is love." Get the mob chanting the catchphrase as you send them off to enact the solution you proposed.

WILD POLITICAL KINGDOM
POLITICAL PARTY MASCOTS

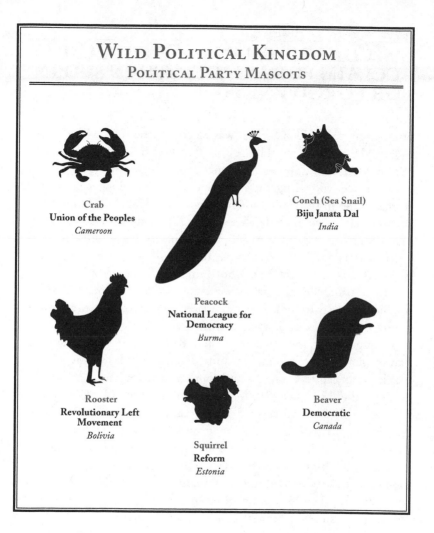

Crab
Union of the Peoples
Cameroon

Conch (Sea Snail)
Biju Janata Dal
India

Peacock
National League for Democracy
Burma

Rooster
Revolutionary Left Movement
Bolivia

Squirrel
Reform
Estonia

Beaver
Democratic
Canada

U.S. CONGRESSMAN WINS POPULAR ACCLAIM FOR MURDER, THEN SCORN FOR FORGIVENESS

A corrupt and bawdy veteran of New York City's Tammany Hall political machine, Dan Sickles was elected to represent Manhattan in the United States House of Representatives in 1857. In Washington, D.C., Sickles, who once took a prostitute as his date to an audience with England's Queen Victoria, plunged into the seamier sides of the capital's social scene. In 1858, he began hearing rumors that his young wife, Teresa, was following his lead by carrying on an affair with lawyer Philip Key. One afternoon, Sickles spotted Key outside his house, waving to his wife with a handkerchief. Sickles confronted Key then shot him in front of dozens of eyewitnesses, firing the third, fatal shot as Key lay on the ground pleading for Sickles to spare him. The subsequent murder trial turned into a media circus. Sickles' lawyer, Edwin Stanton, argued that Sickles was temporarily insane when he shot Key—the first time anyone had employed the temporary insanity defense. Sickles was acquitted. Sickles returned to Congress and found himself a hero, both to the public and to his colleagues, for protecting his honor by killing Key. His political potential seemed almost unlimited, with talk of him running for Senate or even the presidency. But Sickles forgave Teresa the following year and reconciled. His colleagues in Congress began to shun him while voters back home demanded his recall. The Democratic Party refused to re-nominate him, and Sickles returned to New York when his term expired in 1861.

Political Lesson: Forgiveness is not always forgiven.

HOW TO CAMOUFLAGE A BOONDOGGLE

⭐ Slip it into a big bill.
A $5 million boondoggle is much less likely to get noticed if it is folded into a $20 billion spending bill. Insert your boondoggle into big spending measures and budget proposals.

⭐ Time it right.
Introduce your boondoggle as late in the legislative process as possible. Add it as a last-minute rider to a bill that your fellow legislators and the media have already debated and that is certain to pass.

⭐ Team up with a rival.
Gain the support and silence of an opposition legislator by asking him to serve as a co-sponsor. If he is reluctant, cut a deal to co-sponsor one of his boondoggles if he will support your boondoggle.

⭐ Go over the heads of your rival.
If your political rival refuses to help you, finesse your boondoggle's details to benefit some of her big donors and supporters. She will be forced to support your boondoggle or lose support among the people who will benefit from it, meaning you win either way.

*Give the project a prosperous-sounding name
that opponents would be reluctant to challenge.*

★ Tie the project to a larger concern.
Design your boondoggle to appease a prevalent public anxiety. If your project purports to address security concerns in times of war or job creation during economic downturns, more people will get behind it and no one will probably dare to speak out against it.

★ Target the benefits.
Design your boondoggle to benefit a large and powerful segment of your constituency. Get the leadership of large interest groups on board by showing them how they will personally benefit from the project.

★ Give it a prosperous-sounding name.
Christen your project with a title reeking of traditional values and goals shared by a large majority of the population. A title like "The Consumer Security Initiative" or "Local Economic Development Act" will force opponents to think twice before speaking out against it.

★ Create a diversion.
Distract an opponent who might denounce your boondoggle by stirring up a controversy about him. Plant stories in the blogosphere about his alleged personal indiscretions. Alert journalists about questionable donations to his campaign. Raise questions about his relationship with a lobbyist through an e-mail alert to supporters. The controversy will likely divert most of his attention and resources and temporarily undermine your opponent's credibility, making his opposition to your boondoggle less effective.

MASSIVE GOVERNMENT PROJECT TO ALTER WATER FLOW ACROSS NORTH AMERICA

Concocted by a private engineering firm in California in 1964, the North American Water and Power Alliance (NAWAPA) proposed building a series of dams, reservoirs, and canals across three nations and thousands of miles of landscapes. This network of manmade rivers and lakes aimed to divert over 30 trillion gallons of water annually from Northwest Canada into the United States and Mexico. Despite estimates of up to a trillion-dollar price tag and 30-year construction timeline, NAWAPA originally generated great enthusiasm. In 1965, *Newsweek* magazine hailed it as "the greatest, the most colossal, stupendous, super-splendificent public works project in history." Many politicians in the United States supported the scheme and openly lobbied for it. But others began to view NAWAPA in light of its unpredictable and almost unimaginable capacity to disrupt the continent's natural ecosystems. In 1966, after the International Joint Commission reviewed the plan, its head General A.G.L. McNaughton called NAWAPA "a monstrous concept—a diabolical thesis." NAWAPA faded from view in the late 1960s. The NAFTA and WTO trade agreements of the early 1990s made water a commodity that could be moved across international borders, unimpeded by environmental laws and regulations. With water shortages exasperated by population booms in the western United States, some politicians have revisited the plan.

Political Lesson: Times change.

FEEDING AT THE PORK BARREL

Program	Cost	Purpose	Result
The Fast Ferry Fleet British Columbia in Canada	$500 million	To transport people and their cars between Vancouver and Vancouver Island more quickly and reliably than the existing fleet	The new ferries proved slower and less comfortable, as well as prone to breakdown and capsizing, before being sold after a few years for less than 5 percent of what they cost to build.
Cane Toad Introduction Queensland, Australia	Billions of Australian dollars, and rising	To wipe out cane beetle populations plaguing local farmers during the 1930s	The toads ate everything in their path except cane beetles and quickly infested Australia's entire eastern coast while wiping out numerous benign native species and causing billions of dollars of damage.
The Bataan Nuclear Power Plant The Philippines	$2.3 billion	To provide alternative source of power for the Philippines	The plant never generated a single watt of energy and saddled taxpayers with decades of bills for construction costs and debt service.
The Teton Dam The Snake River in Idaho	Over $100 million to construct, over $2 billion to clean up its deconstruction	To provide hydro-electricity, irrigation, and flood prevention	Dam burst shortly after completion, drowning 11 people and thousands of cattle while flooding hundreds of thousands of acres and causing billions in damage.

RUSSIAN BILLIONAIRE PLUMMETS FROM GRACE AFTER GETTING INVOLVED IN POLITICS

By the time he turned 32 years old, Mikhail Khodorkovsky had already become the richest man in Russia with an estimated net worth of over 15 billion U.S. dollars. As owner of the giant Yukos oil company and a founding member of the private sector oligarchy that took over Russia after the fall of communism, Khodorkovsky also enjoyed close relations with the country's governmental and business elite. Because of his vast power and influence, no one questioned the dubious manner in which he'd gained his wealth or just about anything else he chose to do. Khodorkovsky donated money to most of the country's political parties, including the communists. He even financed a new party, the Union of Rightist Forces, dedicated to opposing the policies of the Russian government and Prime Minister Vladimir Putin. Many thought that Khodorkovsky was positioning himself to take over the Russian government. In October 2003, Khodorkovsky was arrested by representatives of the Russian attorney general's office. That same week, Putin froze trading in shares of Yukos, leading to the collapse of the company and Khodorkovsky's fortune. Yukos was charged with tax evasion and forced to forfeit all of its valuable assets to the Russian government. In 2005, Khodorkovsky was convicted of fraud and sentenced to ten years in prison. After the trial, he was transferred from a jail in Moscow to a labor camp in Siberia where prisoners work in a uranium mine and processing plant. Few ever return alive.

Political Lesson: Know when to leave well enough alone.

QUEEN ELIZABETH vs. PRESIDENT OBIANG
OF ENGLAND · OF EQUITORIAL GUINEA

	Queen Elizabeth	President Obiang
Full Name	Elizabeth Alexandra Mary Windsor	Teodoro Obiang Nguema Mbasogo
Position	Queen of the United Kingdom	President of Equatorial Guinea
Gained Through	Inherited throne upon the 1952 death of her father George VI	Took power by killing his uncle and country's ruler Francisco Macias Nguema in 1979 coup
Hold On Power	Granted position for life	Won reelection in 2002 with 100 percent of the vote
Estimated Net Worth	$600 million	$600 million
Gained Through	Inheritance, investment	Drug trafficking, money laundering and skimming nation's oil profits
Entourage	Followed by dozens of paparazzi looking to shoot photo of an embarrassing slip-up	Shadowed by dozens of security officers looking to prevent anyone from shooting him
Housing	Lives in nation's capital of London in Buckingham Palace, which features numerous gardens and over 800,000 square feet of interior space	Lives in nation's capital of Malabo in vast presidential palace that no one outside his inner circle is allowed inside or to even photograph from outside
Perks	Heads Church of England	Regular, direct contact with God and license to kill

HOW TO OPEN AN OFFSHORE BANK ACCOUNT

1 Shop locations.
Make a list of nearby countries with stable governments that you would like to spend time in. Cross off the ones that lack advanced transportation systems to offer you relatively quick and easy access.

2 Check the banking regulations.
Research the laws, regulations, and enforcement practices concerning account reporting, taxes, and international banking laws for each country you are considering.

3 Verify the assets.
Seek banks with long histories and low profiles, significant assets, reputable management teams, and toll-free telephone numbers.

4 Find a secure means of communication.
Obtain a prepaid, disposable cell phone to use exclusively for communicating with your offshore bank candidates. Destroy and replace the phone every few months.

5 Call the banks.
Ask for a roster of depositors. If any of the banks you are considering provides you with this information,

Make a list of countries you would like to spend time in.

cross it off your list. Select your offshore bank from those remaining on the list.

6 Make all your deposits in person.
Do not make deposits electronically or trust anyone to deliver cash to your account. Put the money in a sturdy, lockable briefcase, then handcuff the briefcase to your wrist. Wear long sleeves when traveling.

7 Select a PIN you can remember.

8 Create a cover story.
To prevent people back home from growing suspicious about your frequent trips, establish contacts with the country's trade authorities. Conduct well-publicized meetings in both countries to promote trade between the countries.

Political Brief

Robert Bernard Anderson, U.S. Secretary of the Treasury from 1957–61, owned an illegal offshore bank in the British West Indies. Anderson, who used the unlicensed bank to avoid paying taxes, eventually was discovered and pled guilty to tax evasion and violating U.S. and international banking laws in 1987. He was sentenced to prison.

ILL-GOTTEN GAINS
POLITICIANS AND THE DUBIOUS FORTUNES THEY AMASSED IN OFFICE

A.	**Alfredo Stroessner**	President of Paraguay (1954–89)	$300 million
B.	**William Magear "Boss" Tweed**	Head of the Democratic Party "machine" that ran New York City (from about 1850–72)	$300 million to $3 billion
C.	**Mobutu Sese Seko**	President of Zaire (1965–97)	$5 billion
D.	**Ferdinand Marcos**	President of the Philippines (1966–86)	$5-10 billion
E.	**Mohammad Reza Pahlavi**	Shah of Iran (1941–79)	$10 billion
F.	**Suharto**	President of Indonesia (1967–98)	$15-75 billion

BABY DOC FOLLOWS PAPA DOC'S PRESCRIPTION FOR PLUNDER

Jean-Claude Duvalier—dubbed "Baby Doc" because he was only 19 in 1971 when he assumed control of the Caribbean island nation of Haiti after the death of his father, François "Papa Doc" Duvalier— inspired a brief spike of hope among his constituents when he first came to power. But spurred on by his ruthless wife Michelle Bennett Pasquet, whose family made its fortune in drug and cadaver smuggling, the young Duvalier quickly slipped into his father's pattern of corruption and crushed dissent, murdering tens of thousands of his citizens. He also embezzled an estimated $500 million while his constituents struggled to survive in the Western hemisphere's poorest economy. By October 1985, the citizens of Haiti had seen enough. Popular protests demanding Duvalier's ouster spread across the country and in January 1986, they reached Port-au-Prince, the capital. Fearing for their lives, Duvalier and his family members grabbed as much money and valuables as they could carry and fled to the airport. Just before their plane took off, Duvalier and his wife removed 12 relatives from the plane so their seats could be used to hold more sacks of money and valuables. Duvalier relocated to France and for awhile lived in luxury. But his wife stole most of "his" money, then divorced him. Now bankrupt, Duvalier lives in a borrowed one-bedroom apartment in Paris.

Political Lesson: No matter how awful you are, there's always someone worse.

NATIONS WHOSE ELECTIONS HAVE BEEN OBSERVED BY THE CARTER CENTER

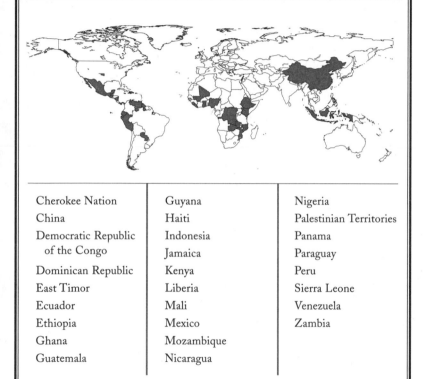

Cherokee Nation
China
Democratic Republic
  of the Congo
Dominican Republic
East Timor
Ecuador
Ethiopia
Ghana
Guatemala

Guyana
Haiti
Indonesia
Jamaica
Kenya
Liberia
Mali
Mexico
Mozambique
Nicaragua

Nigeria
Palestinian Territories
Panama
Paraguay
Peru
Sierra Leone
Venezuela
Zambia

BEWARE OF ENTANGLING ALLIANCES

HOW TO DELIVER A TOAST AT A FORMAL STATE DINNER

1 | **Ask permission to make a toast.**
Before the dinner, approach the host with your request. The host will assign people to deliver toasts to specific people and must inform the guest of honor of what toasts will be proposed and in what order they will take place.

2 | **Determine the right time.**
Plan to make the toast after the main course is finished and just after the dessert wine is served.

3 | **Wait your turn.**
The host must deliver the first toast of the evening. Do not usurp the host's right and privilege or you will be committing the most serious violation of decorum at a formal state dinner, even if you offer a toast in the host's honor.

4 | **Follow the chain of toasts.**
The first toast of the evening honors the head of state of the guest of honor. The guest responds a few minutes later by offering a toast to the head of state of the host country. Everyone in attendance stands during toasts to heads of state. On most occasions, the national anthem of each nation will be played after the toast.

Do not drink excessively before it is your turn to give a toast.

5 | Wait until everyone has a full glass.
Since a toast involves an invitation to drink in someone's honor, it would be rude to initiate the toast before all guests' glasses have been filled with the toasting beverage. Champagne or any dessert wine can be used. It is not appropriate to use a mixed drink or liqueur.

6 | Stand.
Rise to your feet when you make your toast.

7 | Use the right language.
Deliver the toast in the guest of honor's native tongue. If you do not speak that language, do not begin until a translator is present.

8 | Address the guest correctly.
Adhere to proper titles with a salutation like "His Excellency" or "Her Majesty" preceding the title.

9 | Drink.
Even if you don't drink alcohol, raise the glass to your lips. You must go through the motions of participating in the toast and at least pretending to take a sip. Only the person being toasted does not raise her glass to her lips.

FOREIGN FAUX PAS

Country	Faux Pas	Why
Japan	Using the common toasting term "chin chin" when clinking wine glasses	"Chin chin" sounds like Japanese slang for "penis."
Albania	Nodding when you mean "yes"	Symbolizes disapproval in Albania, while shaking your head from side-to-side means "yes."
France	Using the French word "tu" for "you" instead of "vous" when addressing a casual acquaintance	"Tu" is reserved for good friends, family members, and other intimates.
Iraq, Russia, Greece, Australia	Giving someone the "thumbs up" symbol	In many parts of these countries, thumbs up means "up yours."
Ghana	Touching the back of someone's hand	It is considered a bad-luck omen.
Poland	Offering a dinner party host help with preparing a meal or cleaning up	It implies that the host is failing to adequately perform the tasks.
Brazil	Wearing yellow and green in the same outfit	It is considered disrespectful to the yellow and green Brazilian flag.

Political Brief

United States Ambassador to England Charles Dawes caused a diplomatic scandal in 1929 when he refused to wear traditional knee pants for a meeting with King George V, who was already angry at Dawes for his reluctance to introduce him to more young American women.

BEER AND THE HUNGARIAN REVOLUTION

In 1848, liberal reformer Lajos Kossuth led a revolution that established Hungary's first constitution, signaling the country's intent to run its own affairs while remaining part of the Austrian Hapsburg empire. The Austrians attacked, but Kossuth rallied Hungary's military to drive them out of the country. He then declared Hungary completely independent from Austria and its Hapsburg rulers. The following spring, the Hapsburgs recruited their fellow monarchist, Russian Czar Nicholas I, to send reinforcements. The combined Russian and Austrian forces quickly overwhelmed the Hungarian nationalists. Kossuth escaped to Turkey, but many of his fellow revolutionaries were arrested and convicted of treason. Austria's infamous military commander, General Haynau, ordered the execution of the 13 most nationalist leaders. They were hung, one after the other, from a gallows in a public square. After each hanging, the Austrian prison guards celebrated with a beer toast, loudly clanging their glasses together. To protest the executions and obnoxious behavior of the guards, Hungarians unofficially declared a 150-year ban on clanging beer mugs together as a toast. The ban expired in 1999. While the Hungarians touch glasses when toasting with wine or liquor, many still honor their fallen revolutionary heroes by refusing to clink beer glasses. Instead they rap their glass on the table.

Political Lesson: Honor traditions rooted in nationalism.

HOW TO SMUGGLE YOURSELF OUT OF THE COUNTRY

⭐ Avoid changes in routine.
Resist the urge to make your move too abruptly so you don't alert authorities that you are about to escape. Maintain your daily routines while using every spare moment to plot your secret departure. Make sure you camouflage your efforts to gather materials for your escape under the guise of activities that you normally engage in.

⭐ Learn from others' past mistakes.
Review the cases of people that have been arrested for political reasons, focusing on how and where the government made the arrests. Avoid similar circumstances.

⭐ Be wary of unsolicited offers of help.
Rebuke anyone who approaches you about wanting to join or help you with your escape. He may be on assignment from the government to ensnare you.

⭐ Fake them out.
Establish an event in the future that you will be sure to attend. If the government thinks you will be present in the country at least until an upcoming wedding, election, important speech, etc., they will probably wait to

make an arrest in hopes of building their case against you. Just make sure you get out of the country before the event.

★ **Give yourself a head start.**
Begin your escape during a time when others won't notice that you are missing for an extended period, such as a weekend or holiday. The extra time will give you a better chance of making it across the border before the government is aware of your absence.

★ **Use an unexpected route or means of escape.**
Once people notice that you are missing, alerts will go out to authorities along all the likely escape routes and border crossings. If you have to use one of those routes, disguise yourself in an unusual manner. Hide inside a cargo hold containing a common export that needs to be moved quickly such as fruit or another perishable good. Mix in with a group of day laborers heading back across the border. Disguise yourself as a member of the opposite sex. If possible, choose a route that authorities will fail to consider right away. Such routes will probably require longer, more difficult journeys, so be sure to pack everything you need for the trip or arrange to pick up supplies along the way.

Use an unexpected route or means of escape.

NOT SO GREAT ESCAPES

Who	Predicament
Cicero Roman Statesman (1st century BC)	His political enemies, led by his arch-rival Marc Antony, took power in Rome and were executing their foes.
Orkhan Son of Former Sultan Bayazid and Claimant to Throne of Ottoman Empire (1412–53)	Was under house arrest by Byzantine Emperor Constantine when his rival for Ottoman throne Mohammad II invaded and seized control of Byzantine capital Constantinople
Louis XVI King of France (1774–92)	Had been overthrown and put under house arrest
Jefferson Davis President of the Confederate States of America (1861–65)	Union troops had overrun his military, forcing him to dissolve his government and leave the capital.
Antonio López de Santa Anna Commander-in-Chief and President of Mexico (1833–55)	His army had just been routed by Texan revolutionaries at the Battle of San Jacinto.
Nuri Assaid Premier of Iraq under King Faisal II (1939–58)	Faisal was assassinated in a 1958 coup, setting off a general uprising that targeted all high government officials.

Escape	Result
Hid inside his carriage and had servants carry him to the sea to catch a ship to Greece	Overtaken by Antony's men, who cut off his head when he peered out of his carriage; Antony's wife later ripped the tongue out of Cicero's severed head and stabbed it repeatedly for having so often spoken out against her husband
Disguised himself as a Greek monk and attempted to sneak out of the city	Caught and beheaded
Disguised himself as a servant and took a horse-drawn coach, along with his wife and son, toward Austria, where he planned to raise an army and retake France	While passing through a small village, a former servant at Louis's palace recognized him and he was arrested, then later guillotined along with his queen, Marie Antoinette.
Fled southward wearing his wife's cloak and shawl	Captured and imprisoned for two years, during which time he was forced to sell his estate to a former slave
Shed his general's outfit and put on a common soldier's uniform, then tried to slip away through some high grass to a bayou	Caught and taken to a prisoners' encampment, where his soldiers rose up and greeted him as "El Presidente," blowing his cover
Disguised himself as a woman in a veil and burqa	Caught and impaled on a steel pole and abused by mobs, with his corpse left to rot in the street

FUGITIVE NIGERIAN GOVERNOR FLEES

In 1999, Diepreye Alamieyeseigha became governor of Bayelsa, one of Nigeria's most petroleum-rich states. He ruled for the next six years, a period when Nigerian government officials were suspected of embezzling as much as $400 billion from public coffers swelling with money from the nation's oil boom. In 2005, while recuperating from liposuction surgery in England (where he owns an estimated $20 million in real estate), Alamieyeseigha was arrested by British authorities for money laundering. Knowing he would be protected from prosecution by political friends back in his homeland, Alamieyeseigha disguised himself in a dress and wig and used a forged passport to escape England and fly back to Nigeria. When pressed by journalists on how he was able to return home, Alamieyeseigha replied, "My arrival is a mystery. I can't reconcile how I got here. I give God the glory."

Political Lesson: There's no place like home.

Political Brief

In March of 1959, the Dalai Lama, spiritual and political leader of Tibet, fled to India after learning he was about to be arrested by Chinese authorities while attending a theater event they had invited him to. China had invaded Tibet earlier in the decade and had virtually taken over the country. The Lama and a small entourage traveled only by night for 15 days and for over 500 miles through the Himalayan Mountains until crossing the border into India.

HOW TO DISGUISE YOURSELF AS THE OPPOSITE SEX

As a Man

⭐ Shower off perfume.
Scrub off any perfumes or feminine soap smells. Spray on some cologne or male deodorant after drying off.

⭐ Cut your hair.
Shape your hair into a short, masculine style. Cover with a baseball cap or other men's hat.

⭐ Simulate a beard.
Spread burnt cork lightly across your face to help give you a stubbled look.

⭐ Flatten your chest.
Put on a sports bra or tight T-shirt, then wrap a long bandage around your torso several times, starting at the top of your chest and moving downward to push your breasts down. Cover with another T-shirt.

⭐ Sit with legs apart.
Do not cross your legs while sitting. With your feet flat on the ground, leave your knees slightly apart. Alternatively, rest one ankle on the opposite knee. Before going out, practice walking like a man in front of a mirror while wearing men's boots.

⭐ **Rough up your hands.**
Rub your hands with dirt. Trim your nails and remove all nail polish, even clear polish.

⭐ **Cover your neck and arms.**
Unlike women, most men have a protruding Adam's apple and coarse forearm hair. Wear a high collar, long-sleeved shirt, or hooded sweatshirt.

⭐ **Wear oversized clothes.**
Bulky shirts, jeans, sweatpants, or other pants with large pockets will hide your contours.

⭐ **Lower your voice.**
Bring your voice up from deep in your diaphragm. Do not talk about your feelings. Keep your answers short.

⭐ **Look people in the eye.**
Stare directly at people when you are talking to them. This will make it seem like you have nothing to hide and keep them from scrutinizing you for too long.

As a Woman

⭐ **Add a feminine scent.**
Clean yourself thoroughly in a bath with a feminine soap, then lightly scent yourself with a quality brand of perfume.

⭐ **Pluck your eyebrows.**
Get rid of stray hairs and try to achieve a thin, arched brow.

★ | Remove all facial hair.
Shave off all the hair on your neck and face, then shave it again, getting as close as you can to your skin to eliminate all the stubble. Get rid of sideburns. Apply lotion to your face to make your skin moist.

★ | Apply makeup.
Apply a tasteful amount of eyeliner, lipstick, and blush. Avoid foundation covering unless you absolutely need it to cover up stubborn beard stubble—and make sure it matches your natural skin tone. While some makeup will make you look like a woman, too much will make you look like a drag queen.

★ | Fix your hair.
If your hair is long enough, shape it into a typical feminine hairstyle. If your hair is relatively short, use a wig, but only a high-quality one. An ill-fitting wig made of cheap, synthetic material will draw more attention and scrutiny than short hair. If you can't find a good wig, wear a headscarf or a hat with a floppy brim to help cover your face.

★ | Cover your neck.
Use a scarf or turtleneck. Most women, unlike most men, do not have protruding Adam's apples.

★ | Manicure your nails.
Thoroughly wash your hands, removing any dirt underneath the nails. Trim and shape your nails and cover them with a colored polish. Wear a pair of feminine gloves if

your hands are hairy or scarred. If your arms are on the hairier side, shave them or wear a long-sleeved shirt.

⭐ Walk with a wiggle.
Swivel your hips and your shoulders more when you walk. Put more weight on the front instead of the back of your feet. Practice walking in front of a mirror while wearing a good pair of women's shoes.

⭐ Pick out your wardrobe.
Dress to blend in with the other women who will be in your vicinity. Select a dress or outfit that de-emphasizes your biceps, shoulders, and midsection. Add a little padding to approximate feminine curves in the hips, chest, and buttocks. Wear a woman's coat, if weather permits.

⭐ Carry a purse.
Put money and other small items you'll need for your escape into a purse. Add lipstick, a hairbrush, and perfume. Use a purse without a strap so you hold your hands in front of you—a more feminine position than dangling at your sides.

⭐ Cross your legs.
When sitting, place one knee over the top of the other.

⭐ Raise the pitch of your voice.
Close off your throat when you speak so you don't breathe from the diaphragm. Keep your answers short.

Can't Go Home Again

Defector	From	To	Reason
Merujan Artsruni	Armenia	Persia	Fled to Persia in the 360s to protest Armenia's embrace of Christianity and persecution of Zoroastrians like himself
Francisco Javier Mina	Spain	France	Fled to France in 1815 after his failed coup against Spanish King Ferdinand VII
Johann Patkul	Sweden	Switzerland	Fled to Switzerland in 1692 after being accused of treason for protesting the land policies of King Charles XI
Mildred Gillars	United States	Germany	Fell in love with a married German immigrant professor and in 1935 moved from the United States to Nazi Germany, where she worked as infamous radio propagandist "Midge at the Mike" (also known as Axis Sally), taunting American and English forces with predictions of their imminent defeat during World War II
Ndabaningi Sithole	Zimbabwe	United States	Fled to the United States in 1987 after he was politically outmaneuvered by his old ally Robert Mugabe, who became prime minister and had Sithole convicted of conspiracy

SOVIET DOUBLE AGENT VETOES HIS OWN OUTING

Kim Philby was a British intelligence officer really working as a Soviet double agent. In 1945, Konstantin Volkov, a Soviet diplomat based in Turkey, tried to defect to Britain. In exchange for British citizenship, Volkov offered to reveal the identities of two high-ranking British intelligence officers who were working for the Soviets, one of them Philby. As acting head of Britain's Soviet counterintelligence office, Philby was the first to review Volkov's proposition. Volkov mysteriously disappeared from Turkey a short time later and was taken back to the Soviet Union. Soviet authorities questioned Volkov about his defection attempt, then executed him. Philby went on to serve as a double agent for another 18 years before defecting to the Soviet Union in 1963. He was later awarded the Order of the Red Banner for the advancement of communism and the Soviet Union.

Political Lesson: Trust no one.

Political Brief

South Korea began to receive so many defectors from North Korea toward the end of the 20th century that they opened Hanawon, a special resettlement village in the Korean countryside. The facility screened defectors for spies, then offered two months of courses and training on how to transition from life in the impoverished communist North to the capitalist society of South Korea. As defection rates continued to increase, the South Korean government doubled Hanawon's size a few years later.

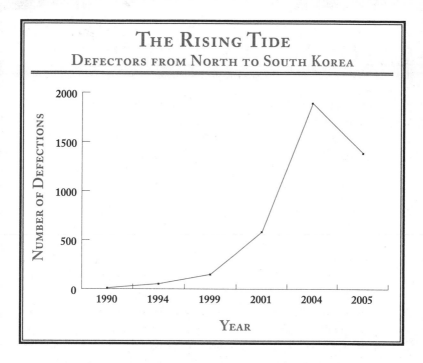

THE RISING TIDE
DEFECTORS FROM NORTH TO SOUTH KOREA

Number of Defections (y-axis): 0, 500, 1000, 1500, 2000

Year (x-axis): 1990, 1994, 1999, 2001, 2004, 2005

Political Brief

United States trade representative Carla Hills often used the metaphor
"prying open a market with a crowbar" to summarize her approach to
international trade negotiations. In 1992, Indian farmers became angry
at Hills and the United States over genetic modification of their native
seeds at a Bangalore factory owned by the U.S. corporation Carghill,
Inc. In a nod to Hills, who had negotiated the controversial treaty that
allowed Carghill to set up shop in the country, 500 Indian farmers took
over the Carghill factory and dismantled it, piece by piece, using crowbars.

DON JUAN ESCOIQUIZ
Foreign Policy Advisor

WORST DEEDS: Convincing his young pupil Prince Ferdinand that his father King Charles IV was going to execute him, infecting Ferdinand with a lifelong case of paranoia ★ Being fired as royal tutor in 1805 for trying to secretly stir up dissent against Spain's alliance with Napoleon and France ★ Attempting to forge his own secret alliance with Napoleon behind the back of King Charles IV in the failed 1807 Escorial Conspiracy ★ Instigating 1808's Mutiny at Aranjuez—a staged popular uprising that tricked King Charles IV to give up his throne to Ferdinand, who appointed Escoiquiz as his top advisor and went on to become perhaps the worst monarch in Spanish history ★ Convincing Ferdinand to join him on an 1808 diplomatic mission to France where both were imprisoned for seven years by Napoleon, who despised their constant conniving and incompetence ★ Gaining another job in 1815 at the Spanish royal court, only to be imprisoned in Spain a short time later for treachery and incompetence ★ Taking a mistress and fathering two children while he was still employed as a priest

BORN: 1762 in Navarre, Spain

DIED: November 27, 1820, in exile

FIRST JOB: Priest

QUOTE: "It is impossible to be more malignant and at the same time more indiscreet and awkward than Escoiquiz"–Manuel de Condoy, Prime Minister of Spain (1792–97, 1801–08) in his memoirs

HOW TO CO-OPT A FOREIGN DIGNITARY

★ **Roll out the red carpet.**
Give the visiting dignitary a grand welcome, with great pageantry that makes him feel important and esteemed. Honor the guest at lavish state dinners and cultural events. Such pomp and circumstance will charm the visitor into feeling more at ease and cooperative, while also distracting from more difficult issues, unfavorable press coverage, and other problems.

★ **Show your influence.**
The more in control that you and your allies appear, the more the dignitary will want to broker substantive deals with you—and make greater concessions to ensure that you accept those deals. Set up events such as parades, special scheduling for football (soccer) games, and other demonstrations of the power you command, and will continue to command for a long time to come.

★ **Take him someplace remote and beautiful.**
After regaling the dignitary in your nation's capital, shuttle him to a remote location in the countryside. Choose someplace quiet and beautiful where you or one of your supporters owns a large home that you can all stay in. Partner with the dignitary in outdoor activities like canoeing or hunting that require cooperation. Take time during the evenings to have informal, one-on-one chats that will allow the dignitary to drop his

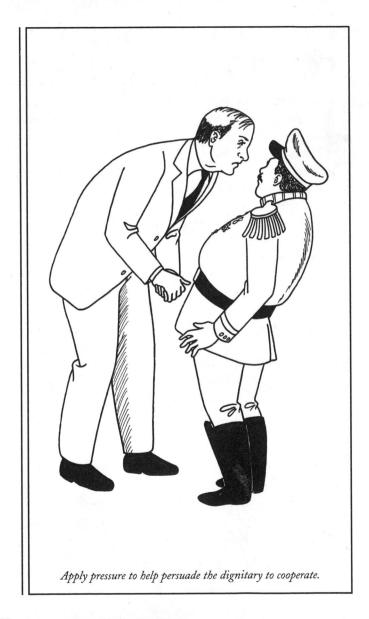

Apply pressure to help persuade the dignitary to cooperate.

public persona and relate to you on a more casual and sincere level.

⭐ Introduce your guest to mind-expanding schemes.
In addition to the usual diplomatic agenda items, discuss exciting new ways in which your two countries can expand their existing relationship. Emphasize the leading role your guest can play in that expansion and how it will greatly benefit both nations. Let the dignitary fill in the blanks on how it will also enhance her political stature and wealth.

⭐ Apply pressure.
Some visiting dignitaries may prove unpleasant and uncooperative no matter what you do during their visit. When it becomes apparent that you are dealing with this type of situation, work to undermine the dignitary's credibility to undermine a potentially negative response or report. Make the dignitary look foolish by taking part in some complex local cultural ceremony, like an ethnic dance or religious ceremony, in which he will have no idea what to do. Sabotage the teleprompter so the media reports the dignitary's gaffes and poor performance.

⭐ Find his or her favorite vice.
Many people become especially susceptible to their vices in foreign lands where they think no one from back home will find out about their indiscretions. Find out which vices may prove most tempting, then subtly make them available. If the dignitary has shown a

propensity for drunkenness or philandering, make available the appropriate alcoholic beverages or social companions.

⭐ **Introduce a new vice.**
Every culture boasts at least a few unique vices that most foreigners have never experienced. Make sure your visitor encounters them.

⭐ **Get it on tape.**
Secretly document your guest's indiscretions with cameras and audio recording equipment. Gracefully, at first, let your guest know what you have. Suggest that your guest might now find a more cooperative attitude to be mutually beneficial. Gradually increase the pressure by suggesting various people who might be interested in seeing the tapes.

Political Brief

Joseph Patrick Kennedy, founder of the liberal Kennedy family American political dynasty, actively lobbied the United States and British governments to pursue greater cooperation with Nazi Germany in the years leading up to World War II. Serving as the United States ambassador to Great Britain, the senior Kennedy repeatedly sought meetings with Adolf Hitler, who refused to meet with him. Kennedy resigned from the ambassador's office in 1940 when U.S. President Franklin Roosevelt ignored his advice and took a more aggressive stance against the Nazis.

NAZI LEADER GOES AWOL IN THE NAME OF PEACE

By the spring of 1941, Adolf Hitler's deputy führer, Rudolph Hess, had become alarmed about his country's future. With Germany preparing to invade the Soviet Union to the east while it continued to battle England on the western front, Hess felt his nation's forces would be spread too thin. But Hess's warnings went unheeded as Hitler ignored him in favor of his aggressive and optimistic generals. A devout occultist, Hess believed that he had been chosen by supernatural forces to save Germany from doom. With the moon aligned with six planets and his personal astrologers assuring him that the day was perfect for his great endeavor, Hess borrowed a German fighter plane and flew northwest on May 10, 1941. Hours later, he parachuted into a farmer's field in Scotland. The farmer detained him until police arrived. Under questioning, Hess insisted that Hitler had sent him to broker a secret peace treaty. British authorities concluded that he was insane. Placed under arrest and subjected to intense psychiatric evaluation, Hess was transferred to West Berlin's Spandau Prison after the war ended. He remained incarcerated there until he died 42 years later.

Political Lesson: Good intentions don't always equal good results.

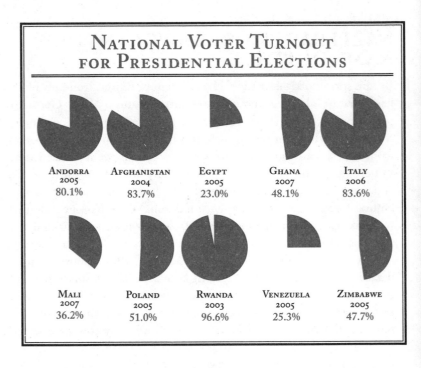

NATIONAL VOTER TURNOUT FOR PRESIDENTIAL ELECTIONS

| ANDORRA 2005 80.1% | AFGHANISTAN 2004 83.7% | EGYPT 2005 23.0% | GHANA 2007 48.1% | ITALY 2006 83.6% |
| MALI 2007 36.2% | POLAND 2005 51.0% | RWANDA 2003 96.6% | VENEZUELA 2005 25.3% | ZIMBABWE 2005 47.7% |

Political Brief

In 1324, Mali emperor Mansa Musa visited Cairo as part of a diplomatic mission to forge better relations with Egypt. During his stay, the wealthy Musa and his followers spent so much gold that the Egyptian currency collapsed, propelling its economy into chaos for over a decade.

COLOMBIAN EFFORT TO IMPROVE UNITED STATES RELATIONS GOES TERRIBLY WRONG

In 2000, United States Senator Paul Wellstone of Minnesota began to voice vigorous concerns about the billions of dollars in annual aid his country provided to Colombia. Wellstone, the Senate's leading champion of human rights, felt that sending money to the corrupt and brutal Colombian government had failed to stem the tide of cocaine coming out of Colombia and had degraded instead of improved the lives of its citizens. Wellstone became particularly concerned about Colombia's program to eradicate its production of illegal drugs by aerially spraying coca, the plant used to produce cocaine. Many Colombian farmers were claiming that government crop dusters were often missing their targets. They said the herbicide was falling onto legal agricultural fields, annihilating their crops and damaging their health. Fishermen said that the herbicide was also drifting into rivers and lakes, killing large swaths of aquatic life and destroying their livelihoods. Upon Wellstone's arrival in June, Colombian officials arranged for a crop dusting demonstration to show how accurate their herbicide applications had become with the help of improved aircraft and satellite imagery. As Senator Wellstone, the United States Ambassador to Colombia, and Colombian officials stood on a hillside overlooking an illegal coca field, a government crop duster flew in for the demonstration. It released its load of herbicide, much of which fell right onto Wellstone and the other dignitaries, soaking their hair and clothing with the toxic chemical.

Political Lesson: Make sure your attempts to impress are well-rehearsed.

POLITICIANS VS. RELIGIOUS LEADERS

Who	Source of Dispute
Henry II, King of England (1154–89) vs. **Archbishop Thomas Becket** (1162–70)	Henry appointed his old friend Becket as Catholic archbishop of Canterbury to help further his efforts to gain more control over the church in England, but Becket became his greatest critic and threatened to excommunicate him.
Frank Church, United States Senator (1957–81) vs. **Jerry Falwell**, Baptist Minister and Co-founder of Political Activist/Religious Group Moral Majority (1979–1989)	Senator Church's support for abortion rights, environmental protection, arms reduction, and the Panama Canal Treaty
Roberto D'Aubuisson, Founder and Head of El Salvador's Ultra-right Wing Nationalist Republican Party (1977–85) vs. **Oscar Romero**, Catholic Archbishop of San Salvador (1977–80)	Brutality of D'Aubuisson's death squads, which had murdered thousands of political opponents, including six Catholic priests that they considered too liberal
Abolhassan Banisadr, President of Iran (1980–81) vs. **Ruhollah Khomeini**, Grand Ayatollah (1979–1989)	Direction of new Islamic government and who would be shaping its policies

Actions Taken	Outcome
Four knights who overheard Henry curse the Archbishop murdered Becket in Canterbury Cathedral.	Outrage over Becket's death forced Henry to give in to the church's political demands and do penance by walking in a sack cloth to Canterbury, where he was flogged by monks.
Moral Majority and Anybody But Church, an offspin group in Church's home state of Idaho, dedicated millions of dollars and hundreds of activists to defeating Church when he was up for reelection in 1980.	Church lost his bid for a fourth term by less than 1 percent of the vote to conservative Steve Symms.
The formerly conservative Romero began using his sermons and other public events to speak out against El Salvador's military and D'Aubuisson's right-wing death squads.	Romero was shot to death by a D'Aubuisson supporter while celebrating mass in 1980; D'Aubuisson was arrested and, though clearly linked to Romero's death, was later released after his backers threatened further violence.
Khomeini ordered the impeachment of Banisadr and the execution of his closest friends and allies.	Banisadr fled the country before he could be arrested and executed; Khomeini appointed his successor and remained the undisputed political and religious leader of Iran until his death.

EMPEROR FORCED TO WAIT SHOELESS IN SNOW FOR AUDIENCE WITH ANGRY POPE

Facing growing internal dissent over his excommunication from the Catholic Church, Holy Roman Emperor Henry IV traveled to northern Italy to meet Pope Gregory VII in January 1077. Henry felt he could negotiate an end to the Investiture Controversy, which began when he refused to allow the pope to appoint his own bishops within the vast Holy Roman Empire. The pontiff made Henry, one of the most powerful people in the world, wait three days outside the castle in the snow, barefoot, with his wife and child before granting him an audience. After finally granting the shivering Henry admission to his castle and making him kneel before him, Gregory lifted his excommunication. But he refused to declare Henry as the legitimate ruler of the Holy Roman Empire. When Henry returned to his capital, he faced a civil war instigated by papal favorite the Duke of Swabia. After Swabia won a key battle in 1080, Pope Gregory excommunicated Henry again—for waging war without his permission. Henry rallied and defeated the rebels. Instead of traveling to Italy with his family to beg Gregory to lift the second excommunication, Henry invaded with his army. He took over Italy in 1081, forcing Pope Gregory to flee the Vatican and go into hiding. Henry installed his own pope in Gregory's place and established himself as the most powerful ruler in Europe.

Political Lesson: Know when to defer and when to defend.

WHO HAD IT WORSE?
JOHN OF PLANO CARPINI VS. JOHN ADAMS

Who	John of Plano Carpini	John Adams
Office	Franciscan Friar	Special Envoy
From	Lyon, France	Boston, Massachusetts, United States
To	Karakorum, Mongolia	Paris, France
Miles	Approximately 4,500 miles	Approximately 4,700 miles
By	Horse and on foot	Ship
Obstacles	Harsh weather, bandits, mountains, wide, icy rivers	Harsh winter weather, lightning strike, pirate attack, scurvy
Left On	April 16, 1245	February 5, 1778
Arrived	July 17, 1246	April 1, 1778
Sent By	Pope Innocent IV	United States Congress
Mission	Get Mongolia's Great Khan Guyuk to allow Christianity into his kingdom, then convert him to Christianity and use his new faith to convince him to call off the Mongol invasion of Europe	Negotiate military alliance between the United States and France
Result	Guyuk revealed Christianity had already reached Mongolia but he refused to convert; he then asserted he was ruler of the whole world, including Europe, and ordered Carpini to turn around and go home.	Upon arriving, Adams learned that an alliance between France and the United States had already been negotiated and signed before he had even set sail.

REBEL GROUP TRIES TO WIN FREEDOM FOR IRELAND BY TAKING CANADA HOSTAGE

The Fenian Brotherhood formed in the United States in the 1850s as an expatriate Irish militia dedicated to forcing the British out of Ireland. Hundreds of Fenians enlisted in the U.S. Civil War with the specific goal of gaining military training. Many then returned to Ireland to participate in an armed rebellion, but English authorities learned of the plot and detained most rebels shortly after they got off the boats. As a result, the Fenians remaining in America decided to conquer Canada, then hold it hostage until the British left Ireland. In 1866, about 25,000 Fenian soldiers invaded various parts of Canada, then still a collection of English colonies, but they were forced to return when the U.S. military cut off their supply lines. The U.S. government confiscated the retreating Fenians' weapons and made them promise to abandon their endeavor. A small group of Fenians broke their promise and reorganized to again invade Canada in 1870, but they turned back at the first sign of resistance. Another excursion into Manitoba the next year ended almost as quickly. The Fenians next commissioned an Irish submarine designer, John Holland, to build a submarine with the idea of attacking British merchant and navy vessels in North America. Unable to pay for the sub, named *Fenian Ram*, the Feinians stole it, but soon realized that it was useless without Holland's instructions, which were understandably not forthcoming.

Political Lesson: If it sounds like a bad idea, it probably is a bad idea.

ENCORE
ACTORS WHO HAD A SECOND CAREER IN POLITICS

Who	As Politician(s)	As Actor(s)
Jarosław and Lech Kaczyński	Lech is the current president of Poland while Jarosław served as its prime minister from 2006-07	At the age of 12, the identical twins starred as a pair of greedy bullies in the 1962 movie *The Two Who Stole the Moon*
Glenda Jackson	Representative in England's Parliament since 1992	Twice nominated for the Academy Award as Best Actress for her roles as the sex–addicted spouse of composer Peter Tchaikovsky in 1970's *The Music Lovers* and as a woman carrying on an adulterous affair in 1973's *A Touch of Class*
Jesse Ventura	Governor of Minnesota (1999–2003)	Performed for over a decade as the vain, feather-boa-wearing pro-wrestling villain Jesse "The Body" Ventura. Prior to being elected, he starred in the films *Predator* and *The Running Man*, both opposite actor-turned-politician Arnold Schwarzenegger
Michael Cashman	Member of European Parliament from England (1999–)	Appeared on the BBC series *EastEnders* from 1986–89 as Colin Russell, the first male character on daytime television in Britain to kiss another man
Ronald Reagan	U.S. President (1981–89)	Acted in dozens of films, including the 1951 comedy *Bedtime for Bonzo*, in which he costarred with a chimp
Arnold Schwarzenegger	Governor of California (2003–)	Starred in 1984's *The Terminator* as a cyborg time-traveling back to kill the mother of a populist revolutionary
Hideo Higashikokubau	Governor of Miyazaki in Japan (2007–)	Popular comedian who acted in the film sex comedy *Getting Any?* and served as the host of the TV game show Takeshi's Castle

WALKING THE PLANK
ACTORS WHO HAVE MOVED FROM
TV's *The Love Boat* INTO POLITICS

Who	Love Boat Role	Political Role
Fred Gandy	Played series regular Burl "Gopher" Smith, the ship steward, from 1977–84	U.S. Representative from Iowa (1987–95)
Gavin MacLeod	Starred as Captain Merrill Stubing throughout the series run from 1977–86	Current mayor of Pacific Palisades, California
Sonny Bono	Guest-starred on 1979 episode "Sounds of Silence" as lonely heavy metal rock-star Deacon Dark and as Steve Bloom on "Pride of the Pacific" episode in 1982	U.S. Congressman from California (1995–98)
Nancy Kulp	Had recurring role as Aunt Gert in episodes from 1978–81	Ran as Democratic candidate for Congress vs. incumbent Republican Bud Shuster of Pennsylvania in 1984, but lost
Maureen Reagan	Played Mrs. Moss on the "Ship of Ghouls" episode in 1978	Right–wing political talk-show host and activist, daughter of U.S. President Ronald Reagan (1981–89)
Ruth Warrick	Guest starred on 1982's "Man in the Iron Shorts" episode	Education consultant to President Kennedy's Department of Labor and President Lyndon Johnson's Job Corps and member of U.N.'s World Women's Committee

SEXTUS POMPEY
Political Dissident

WORST DEEDS: Becoming a dissident leader in the rebellion against Julius Caesar after Caesar overthrew his father and the Roman Republic in 48 BC ★ Turning to piracy himself after Caesar defeated his rebel army ★ Taking over Sicily and using it as a base to assemble a vast pirate fleet to prey on Roman military and commercial vessels ★ Bringing Italy to the brink of famine and causing riots in Rome by raiding most of the ships carrying grain to Italy ★ Negotiating control of Sicily, Sardinia, and part of Greece and the political position of consul from Rome in return for ceasing his pirate activities ★ Resuming his pirating after declaring the part of Greece he was granted insufficient ★ Inspiring Roman rivals Octavian and Marc Antony to declare a truce so they could join forces to rid the Mediterranean of him ★ Defeating his former countrymen in numerous naval battles and skirmishes ★ Finally losing his fleet in battle to Roman general Marcus Agrippa in 36 BC and fleeing to Asia Minor

BORN: Date unknown

DIED: 35 BC after being captured and executed by Antony's agents, causing dissent even in death as the "illegal" execution gave Octavian pretense to end his alliance with Antony

FAMILY: Father: Pompey the Great, the Roman political and military leader who wiped out the pirate fleets that controlled the Mediterranean in the summer of 66 BC

NICKNAME: Big Patriot

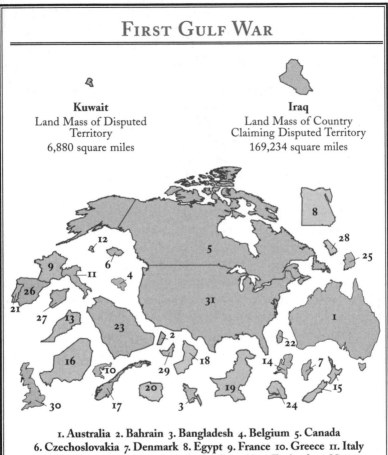

FIRST GULF WAR

Kuwait
Land Mass of Disputed
Territory
6,880 square miles

Iraq
Land Mass of Country
Claiming Disputed Territory
169,234 square miles

1. Australia 2. Bahrain 3. Bangladesh 4. Belgium 5. Canada
6. Czechoslovakia 7. Denmark 8. Egypt 9. France 10. Greece 11. Italy
12. Kuwait 13. Morocco 14. Netherlands 15. New Zealand 16. Niger
17. Norway 18. Oman 19. Pakistan 20. Poland 21. Portugal 22. Qatar
23. Saudi Arabia 24. Senegal 25. South Korea 26. Spain 27. Syria 28. Turkey
29. United Arab Emirates 30. United Kingdom 31. United States of America

Total Land Mass of Coalition Countries Aligned
to take back Kuwait from Iraq
16,322,242 square miles

DISPUTED ISLANDS

Island	Claimed by
Faroe Islands	Ireland, Vikings, Norway, Denmark, England, sovereign independence
Malta	Phoenicians, Carthage, Rome, Byzantine, Arabs, Siculo-Normans, Knights of Malta England, sovereign independence
Puerto Rico	Ortiroids, Igneri, Taino, Spain, sovereign independence, United States
Sri Lanka	Veddahs, Sinhalese, Tamil, Portugal, Netherlands, England, Independence, Tamils and Sinhalese in civil war (1983)
Spratly Islands	Nanyue Kingdom, China, Vietnam, France, Indonesia, Malaysia, Philippines, Brunei
Marshall Islands	Micronesia, Spain, Germany, Japan, United States, sovereign independence

DISPUTE CREATES OPPORTUNITIES FOR SEDUCTIVE MEDIATOR

In 1727, French Guiana and Dutch Guiana invited Portuguese soldier and diplomat Lt. Colonel Francisco de Melo Palheta from Brazil to help them resolve a dispute. The two European colonies had been battling for years over the exact location of the boundary between them in northeastern South America. Unbeknownst to his French Guianan hosts, Palheta arrived at the peace conference with his own secret agenda—to steal a coffee plant. At the time, the French ranked as world leader in the growing world coffee trade, with large plantations in their warm weather colonies, including French Guiana. But they guarded their resource jealously. The Portuguese had often requested that the French give them coffee plants to propagate the plant in Brazil. But the French, who had gained their first coffee plant only after long negotiations between their King Louis XIV and the Dutch, always refused. Upon arriving in French Guiana, Palheta noted the tight security around the coffee plantations, which were walled off and patrolled by armed guards. He then seduced the wife of French Guiana's governor, carrying on an affair with her until he had successfully negotiated a settlement over the border dispute. As he was leaving, she handed him a bouquet of flowers, ostensibly as an official gesture of gratitude for his diplomatic success. Knowing Palheta had been trying to obtain a coffee plant, she hid several unroasted coffee beans in the bouquet. Upon returning to Brazil, Palheta turned the beans over to botanists. By the end of the century, Brazil grew more coffee than any country in the world and enjoyed a virtual monopoly in the coffee industry by the middle of the 19th century.

Political Lesson: Use your opportunities wisely.

CROSSING THE LINE
ONGOING BORDER DISPUTES

Disputed Area	Countries	Status
The David Gareja Monastery	Georgia and Azerbaijan	Despite over 15 years of negotiations, both countries still claim ownership of the mountaintop complex.
Parts of the Atacama region	Bolivia and Chile	After the Saltpeter War (1879–83), Chile annexed part of Peru along with part of the Atacama Desert. Bolivia continues to claim ownership of the Atacama and a path to the sea.
Banc du Geyser, a reef off the coast of Madagascar that remains submerged beneath the Indian Ocean except during low tides	France, Madagascar, and Comoros	Madagascar annexed the reef in 1976, but speculation about possible offshore oil reserves nearby has fueled the interest of the other two countries.
Gibraltar, tip of Iberian Peninsula	Spain and Great Britain	In 1967, Gibraltar's residents voted 12,138 to 44 in favor of remaining a British territory, but the Spanish continue to press their claim.
Imia and Kardak, two tiny islets in the Aegean Sea	Turkey and Greece	While a cease-fire was established, ownership of the islets still remains in dispute.

POWER OUTAGE

HOW TO ESCAPE ASSASSINATION BY NINJA

1 | Block thrown objects and projectiles.
Use a briefcase or duck behind the podium to block the ninja's *shuriken* (bladed throwing stars), and darts from a *fukiya* (blowgun) blown from the ninja's mouth.

2 | Avoid the ninja's hands and feet.
Wield the end of a long implement such as a microphone stand or flagpole to keep your distance from the ninja's *kakute* (spiked ring), *neko-te* (iron fingernails), and *ashiko* (footclaw).

3 | Create confusion.
Toss loose papers, pens, breath mints, and campaign buttons at the ninja's face to confuse his vision and ability to track your movements. If you have a laser pointer, beam it at the ninja's eyes.

4 | Roll.
Duck and roll across the stage and away from the attack to stay beneath the ninja's *metsubushi* (small sand-filled explosives or projectiles used to blind).

Wield the end of a microphone stand to keep the ninja's hands and feet at bay.

5 Cover the ninja.

Pull down a stage curtain or yank free a tablecloth. Throw it over the ninja. This will slow his movements and block his vision long enough to allow your escape.

6 Run.

Do not attempt to fight the ninja. Once he has lost the element of surprise and the immediate first engagement has passed, he will retreat from open public environments.

Be Aware

• Ninjas depend on their stealth to gain advantage over their target. Once you have spotted the ninja, you have erased this advantage.

• At public appearances, avoid standing in or near areas of predominantly dark solid color or shadow, both of which are favored by ninjas.

• Ninjas cannot walk on water, nor can they fly, walk through walls, change their shape, or rise from the dead. These are all myths silently encouraged by ninjas to enhance their reputations.

• Carry a small can of hairspray and a cigarette lighter, which together can be used as a flamethrower to defend against a ninja attack.

Ducked Assassination Attempts

Who	Assassination Attempt
Alexander II, Czar of Russia (1855–81)	Survived five assassination attempts between 1866–81
Teddy Roosevelt, U.S. President (1901–09)	Shot in chest in 1912, with the bullet losing terminal velocity as it passed through his steel glasses case and a copy of a speech, which he delivered a few minutes later while still bleeding
Jean Chrétien, Canadian Prime Minister (1993–2003)	A knife-wielding assassin showed up at the prime minister's residence, and Chrétien and his wife prepared to defend themselves until security arrived
Margaret Thatcher, British Prime Minister (1979–1990)	The IRA planted a bomb in her hotel room in Brighton, England, during a Conservative Party conference. Thatcher was in the bathroom and escaped the bomb.
Pervez Musharraf, President of Pakistan (2001–)	Assassin fired an anti-aircraft missile at his plane, barely missing, in 2007
Alfred Ernest Albert, Prince of Saxe-Coburg and Gotha (1844–1900)	Shot in the back while attending a charity picnic
Ronald Reagan, U.S. President (1981–89)	Shot by a lone gunman as he was leaving a Washington, D.C., hotel

CASTRO DODGES HUNDREDS OF ASSASSINATION ATTEMPTS

Fearing a communist regime only 90 miles from their shores, the United States government's Central Intelligence Agency began attempting to assassinate the new Cuban leader shortly after he came to power in 1959. Over the course of the next four decades, the CIA attempted to kill Castro 638 times, by the estimates of Castro's security chief. Their failed efforts included everything from a poisoned handkerchief to an exploding cigar. They even plotted to eliminate Castro, an avid scuba diver, with a booby-trapped mollusk designed to blow up as he swam past. In 1960, frustrated in their early failures, the CIA turned to the Mafia for help. Castro had closed down the mob's lucrative gambling operations in Havana shortly after taking power, and they were happy to oblige. Despite the efforts of this unusual, unofficial, and short-lived alliance, the desired result was not achieved. The CIA continued trying to kill Castro, attempting as late as 2000 to eliminate him with an exploding podium while he gave a speech in Panama. Castro remains alive as of 2008, although he retired from power in February of that year.
Political Lesson: Your enemy's enemy may become your friend, but not for long.

Political Brief

United States President James Garfield (1831–81) died of blood poisoning almost three months after being shot by an assassin. The infection was likely caused by doctors trying to pull the bullet out of his chest without first sterilizing their hands.

WORST POLITICAL DEATHS

Who	Death
Sani Abacha President of Nigeria 1993–98	Died of a Viagra overdose in bed with two prostitutes
Nitaro Ito Candidate for Japanese House of Representatives 1979	Stabbed himself in the thigh so he could claim he fought off attackers and generate publicity, but hit an artery and bled to death
Brahim Deby Eldest Son and Top Advisor, 2004–06, of Chad's President Idriss Deby	Asphyxiated by attackers who squirted a fire extinguisher down his throat
Edmund II "Ironside," King of England April–November 1016	Felled by an assassin who hid in his bathroom, then jumped out and stabbed him while he was on the toilet
Frederick I Holy Roman Emperor 1155–90	Drowned after jumping into a river to refresh himself after a long march, but without first taking off his heavy armor
Edward II King of England 1307–27	Angered by his bisexuality, Edward's wife had her aides heat a long steel rod in a fireplace, then shove it into his rectum
Great She Elephant Ntombazi Queen of Ndwande Tribe until 1805	Captured by her son's rival Shaka Zulu, Ntombazi was locked in a house with a pack of wild hyenas, who ripped her apart and ate her
Sir Billy Snedden Speaker of the House in Australian Parliament 1976–83	Died of a heart attack in a motel while having sex with his son's girlfriend

HOW TO WRITE A BEST-SELLING MEMOIR

1 Determine your most salable secrets.
Review your political career and consider all the sensitive, secret, private, or scandalous information or events you have knowledge of or have taken part in. Determine which of these events are likely to be of the keenest interest to the public, but that you may reveal without significantly tarnishing your reputation or legacy. Use these scandals and revelations to market and drive interest in your memoir.

2 Settle old scores.
Political memoirs published at the end of a career of public service are ideal platforms for settling old scores and lashing out at those with whom it was important to stay on collegial terms while in office, but whom you are now free to criticize without recourse. Human nature ensures that common interest in gossip and conflict will help boost attention for the book.

3 Overcome adversity.
Start the memoir with stories of you overcoming a tough beginning and numerous obstacles as you rise to prominence. If you have never struggled with adversity, begin your story with hardships suffered by your parents, grandparents, or ancestors. Portray yourself as having learned valuable lessons from these struggles.

Apply your political campaign skills to promote your memoir.

4 | Lay claim to accomplishments.
Take credit for all positive events that occurred during your time in office and attribute them to your actions or conscious inaction. Also claim credit for avoiding negative events that did not come to pass.

5 | Attribute failures.
List personal, political, national, and international failures and disappointments during your time in office and attribute them to political adversaries.

6 | Optimize the timing of the book's release.
Play off current events, such as upcoming elections, especially if you are planning on revealing negative information about a candidate. This will drive news coverage and sales of your book.

7 | Leak juicy details.
Choose a few scandalous details or assertions and reveal them to the media just before publication.

8 | Include a big index.
People will buy the book if they think they're mentioned.

9 | Promote.
Apply your political campaign skills to promote your memoir. As with your campaigns, promise the audience more than you actually deliver.

RACIST POLITICIAN CHANGES CAREER, RACE, WRITES BOOK

Eighteen years before he became a famous Native American children's author, Caucasian Asa Earl Carter ran for lieutenant governor of Alabama in 1958 on a white supremacy platform. He finished last, but his talent for rhetoric won him a speechwriting job for George Wallace, who delivered Carter's famous "Segregation now! Segregation tomorrow! Segregation forever!" at his inauguration as Alabama's governor in 1963. But as Wallace looked toward a run at the presidency, Carter accused him of losing touch with his Alabama constituents. Carter ran against Wallace for governor in 1970, promising to end racial integration in Alabama, but received less than 2 percent of the vote. In 1973, Carter moved to Florida, where he acquired a deep tan and a new racial identity. Calling himself "Forrest" Carter, the former white supremacist now claimed he was a Cherokee Indian storyteller. Carter, who wrote with a bottle of whiskey and a loaded gun next to his typewriter, cemented his new identity with *The Education of Little Tree*, a childhood "memoir" purportedly recounting how Carter's Cherokee grandparents and a kind Jewish neighbor taught him to live in harmony with nature and other people. Released in 1976, the book garnered rave reviews. Later that year, the *New York Times* published an exposé on Carter's racist political career and his true family history. Carter began to drink even more heavily, and died in 1979 from choking on his own vomit after a drunken brawl with his son.

Political Lesson: Once you run for public office, your private life becomes public property.

AFTER-OFFICE JOBS

Who	Office	Later Job
Roy Blanton	Governor of Tennessee (1975–79)	Used car salesman
Zafarullah Khan Jamali	Prime Minister of Pakistan (2002–04)	Chairman of the Pakistan Hockey Federation
Cincinattus	Roman Dictator (5th century BC)	Farmer
Jerry Springer	Mayor of Cincinnati (1977–78)	Host of daytime TV tabloid talk show
Chandragupta Maurya	Founder and Emperor of Maurya Dynasty in India (322–298 BC)	Hermit who starved himself to death in a cave while meditating
Mikhail Gorbachev	Leader of the Soviet Union (1985–91)	Spokesmodel for Pizza Hut and Louis Vuitton handbags
Valentine Strasser	Dictator of Sierra Leone (1992–96)	Unemployed and living with his mother

HOW TO ENSURE YOUR LEGACY

★ Appoint relatives to positions of power.
Have close family members and other relatives assume your own and other positions of power, both to continue with your own agendas and to be in a position to protect and burnish your reputation.

★ Erect statues in your likeness.
Direct funds to create statues and sculptures of yourself and place them at historic or political points or central outdoor gathering spots. Ensure that some feature you riding horseback.

★ Issue currency and stamps in your likeness.
Replace the image on a current currency denomination or issue a new denomination featuring a portrait of you in a heroic context. Be sure that the denomination that you choose is not of such low value that you are associated with the purchase of cheap items, but not so high in value that the bill is rarely seen in circulation. Issue postage stamps bearing similar portraits of yourself.

★ Create a museum and library of your life and work.
Direct funds to the construction of a monumental museum and library complex dedicated to your celebration, placed centrally in the most popular and historic park in the capital city. Deposit non-incriminating paperwork and quaint personal items.

Rename existing streets, parks, and airports in your honor.

★ Rename everyday places and things.
Add your name to streets, parks, schools, bridges, airports, cities, a breed of dog, variety of flower, signature cocktail, or day of the week.

★ Declare a holiday in your honor.
Announce that your birthday is now an annual national holiday. Give everyone the day off.

★ Appoint yourself "Eternal Leader."
Give yourself an honorific title that is a step above the office you are leaving and that your successor will hold, and that is not subject to election, replacement, or succession.

Political Brief

After falling from power, Jean Bedel Bokassa, emperor of the Central African Empire from 1976–79, was placed on trial for murder, corruption, treason, and cannibalism. The charges stemmed, in part, from an incident in which about 100 school-children had been killed, then eaten, for protesting a mandate that they purchase expensive school uniforms from Bokassa's government. Bokassa died in prison in 1996.

SHORTEST TENURES/REIGNS IN OFFICE

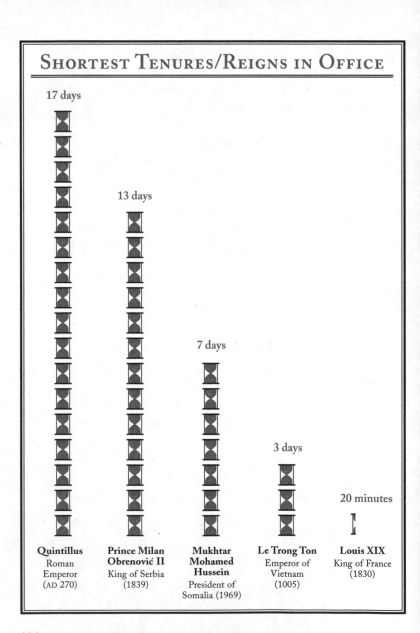

17 days

13 days

7 days

3 days

20 minutes

Quintillus
Roman
Emperor
(AD 270)

**Prince Milan
Obrenović II**
King of Serbia
(1839)

**Mukhtar
Mohamed
Hussein**
President of
Somalia (1969)

Le Trong Ton
Emperor of
Vietnam
(1005)

Louis XIX
King of France
(1830)

HOW PANAMA BECAME A COUNTRY AND GOT A CANAL

Trained and hired as an engineer by France's Panama Canal Company in 1884, Frenchman Philippe-Jean Bunau-Varilla maneuvered his way to the head of the organization within months. The company was attempting to build a canal through Central America that would shear 8,000 miles off the journey for ships traveling between the Atlantic and Pacific Oceans. But under Varilla's leadership, the company went bankrupt after only three years due to massive fraud and mismanagement. The New Panama Canal Company subsequently launched by Varilla also lurched toward bankruptcy. Varilla then turned to the United States, which was planning to build its own canal through Nicaragua. Varilla began an anti-Nicaraguan lobbying effort, sending every United States senator a postcard showing Nicaragua's Mount Momotombo spewing lava near the proposed canal site. Convinced that Nicaragua was geologically unstable, the U.S. Senate voted in 1902 to designate the Panamanian isthmus as its preferred canal site and pledging over $800 million to the effort. But the Panamanian isthmus remained part of Colombia, which refused to allow the United States to use it for a canal. So Varilla drafted a plan for the War of Panamanian Independence, complete with a new flag and constitution. He persuaded President Roosevelt to send a U.S. warship to block the Colombian navy from delivering soldiers to Panama, then launched his "revolution"—which consisted largely of Varilla and a few friends riding a fire truck down the main street of the nation's new capital. Varilla then took it upon himself to travel to Washington, D.C., and sign a treaty ceding control of the Panama Canal Zone to America. Varilla returned to France and the United States built the canal over the next decade.

Political Lesson: Don't underestimate the power of persistence.

POLITICAL TRIBUTES

Who	Tribute
Tamerlane Head of Timurid Dynasty, 1370–1405	Pyramid built from 70,000 skulls of prisoners of war he had beheaded
Woodrow Wilson and Grover Cleveland U.S. Presidents, 1913–31; 1885–89 and 1893–97	Rest stops on the New Jersey Turnpike
Leopold II King of Belgium, 1865–1909	Belgian crowds booed his corpse during Leopold's funeral parade
Elagabalus Roman Emperor, AD 218–222	Giant statue of his phallus in Rome
Saparmurat Niyazov Ruler of Turkmenistan, 1985–2006	New variety of melon
Susan B. Anthony 19th-century U.S. political activist	A $1 coin (The design flaws made it so unpopular, U.S. mints ceased production a year after its debut.)
Eva Perón First Lady of Argentina, 1946–52	Husband Juan Perón preserved her corpse, propping it up in a chair for meals and parties
Victor Emmanuel First King of Unified Italy, 1861–78	Huge structure in Rome whose awkward form and bright white hue inspired locals to rename it "The False Teeth"

BRIDGE ADVOCATED BY EARLY NAZI HELPS ALLIES TAKE DOWN HITLER

A highly respected German general, Erich Ludendorff pushed for the construction of a bridge across the Rhine River at Remagen. Named in his honor, the Ludendorff Bridge expedited the movement of soldiers and supplies out of Germany to the western front in France during World War I. Following the the war, Ludendorff went on to become an early champion of Adolf Hitler. The esteemed general's support helped legitimize the Nazi Party and the eventual German dictator. He participated in the Nazis' infamous 1923 Beer Hall Putsch, Hitler's first effort to seize control of Germany. But Ludendorff eventually became disillusioned with Hitler and withdrew from public life before dying in 1937. In 1945, as Allied forces advanced toward Germany from the West, Hitler ordered the destruction of all the bridges across the Rhine. But due to some malfunctioning detonators, the Ludendorff Bridge at Remagen remained intact. The American army took the bridge after a fierce battle, knowing it was the only remaining link across the Rhine into Germany. The bridge proved invaluable, as Allied soldiers, tanks, and supplies streamed across it. With the Allies in pursuit, the Germans didn't have enough time to establish solid new defensive fronts and were forced to keep retreating. The Ludendorff Bridge collapsed from structural damage three weeks after the battle. But by then Allies had used it to anchor the construction of a new bridge, allowing for continued movement of supplies and soldiers to press the German retreat and hasten the collapse of the Nazi government a few months later.

Political Lesson: Sometimes you should make sure to burn your bridges.

HOW TO
DRIVE A TANK

1   Survey the area.
Evaluate the immediate surrounding area before entering the tank, since the field of vision is limited once inside. Note obstacles or unstable ground and steep slopes or banks, which can cause the vehicle to roll.

2   Board the tank.
Use the skirt step on the left front of most tanks to climb onto the front of the tank. Locate the driver's hatch, below the turret. Lift and swing the hatch to the side, locking it in the open position. Climb inside. Close and lock the hatch behind you.

3   Sit down.
The driver's seat, located in the center of the space, is tilted back like a dentist's chair to accommodate the driving area's low ceiling. Adjust the angle and height of the seat until you are comfortable and can see through the periscopes directly in front of your seat and can reach the controls.

4   Identify the gauges and instruments.
Your driver's master control panel sits to your right and instrument panel to your left. The instrument panel features your fuel level indicator and other gauges while the control panel holds the switches and knobs necessary to turn on the tank's engines, fans, and other systems. The controls and gauges are clearly marked.

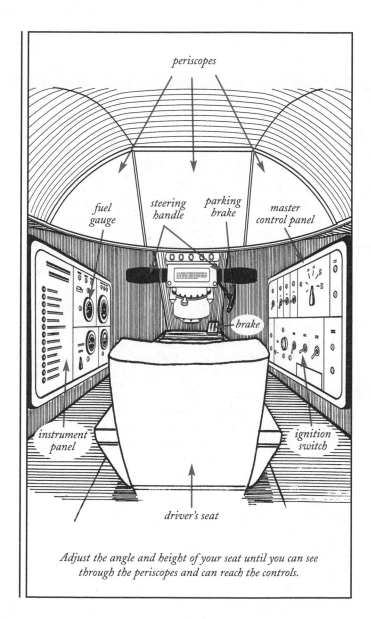

periscopes

fuel gauge

steering handle

parking brake

master control panel

brake

instrument panel

ignition switch

driver's seat

Adjust the angle and height of your seat until you can see through the periscopes and can reach the controls.

The gearshift is located atop the steering handle in front of you.

5 | Check the fuel gauge.
Examine the fuel gauge on the instrument panel to your left to determine whether you have enough fuel to start the tank and reach your destination. Tank fuel consumption is measured in gallons per mile. You will need 10 gallons just to start the engine and about two gallons per mile once you get going. You can travel about 300 miles on a full tank of fuel.

6 | Start the tank.
Flip the silver ignition switch at the bottom left-center of your control panel up to the "On" position. The engine will need about three to five minutes to warm up. You can help speed the process by revving the engine, twisting back the throttle on the right steering grip as you would on a motorcycle grip.

7 | Test the periscopes.
The driver's visual system consists of three periscopes that look like windshields. The two on either side of you allow you to view in front of the tank and to its left and right for about a 120-degree visual field. In between those two periscopes, you will find a central image-intensifying periscope, which looks straight ahead, for use in driving at night or in smoky or dusty situations.

8 | Release the parking brake.
The parking brake control is to the right of your steering handle. Pull on its black, T-shaped handle, twist, and ease it downward to release it.

9 | Put the tank into gear.
Pull the silver transmission selector knob above the steering handle and ease it into the D (Drive) slot, second from the right.

10 | Start slowly.
Some tanks can accelerate from 0 to 45 mph in under ten seconds. Ease the throttle back to move ahead, slowly at first, twisting back further as you feel more comfortable with handling the tank at higher speeds.

11 | Steer.
Guide the tank as you would a bicycle, snowmobile, or motorcycle by rotating the steering handlebar to the left and right.

12 | Listen for tread buildup.
The tank's treads can become disabled with debris. If the tank is not responding quickly to your steering, you may have mud, sand, or some other substance built up on your tracks, which can cause the treads to come off the wheels, leaving the tank essentially immobilized. This buildup is usually accompanied by a popping sound. Drive the tank forward in a straight line over level ground until the popping stops, indicating that the tracks have cleared themselves.

13 Brake.

Once you have arrived at your destination, come to a stop by easing your foot all the way down on the service brake located on the floor beneath your steering handle. Before exiting the tank, re-apply the parking brake by pulling the black T-shaped handle to your right.

Be Aware

- Put on protective headgear before entering the tank. Tank interiors are full of levers, knobs, and other protruding objects that can cut, burn, or daze.
- Never try to get onto and into a tank while it is in motion, no matter how slowly it is moving.
- Wear earplugs or noise-canceling headphones. Tank engines are loud.
- Run the exhaust fan for at least five minutes for every hour on board to replenish the tank's limited oxygen supply.
- Tank interiors can be claustrophobic and nauseating, as they tend to fill with overpowering odors from their huge engines. Skip your previous meal before your tank ride.

PAUL ANKA HELPS THWART PHILIPPINES' COUP ATTEMPT

Corazon Aquino hoped to usher in a new populist era in the Philippines when she replaced the corrupt authoritarian Ferdinand Marcos as her country's president in 1986. But Marcos' old cronies and factions within the nation's military led bloody anti-Aquino demonstrations, almost daily calls for her resignation, and a string of coup attempts. Aquino sought to stabilize the country and her position by holding a national referendum in February 1987 on a newly drafted constitution. A few days before voters went to the polls, however, 250 mutinous army soldiers and officers took over Channel 7, a TV and radio station in suburban Manila. They began broadcasting calls for a national uprising against Aquino. More than a thousand soldiers loyal to Aquino surrounded the Channel 7 building, but they balked at storming the station. They feared that an attack would create martyrs for the anti-Aquino forces and further fracture loyalties within the military. To ease the tensions and promote harmony, Aquino's forces set up dozens of amplifiers around Channel 7. They then blasted the rebels with sentimental pop music, including heavy doses of Paul Anka, whose song "Oh, What A Lonely Boy" was played over and over again at high volume. After three days, the rebels laid down their arms and surrendered. Overwhelmed by the good feelings of the moment, they performed a "three cheers for democracy" chant and exchanged well wishes with Aquino's soldiers. The new constitution was approved by a wide majority. Corazon Aquino remained president of the Philippines until stepping down on her own accord in 1992.

Political Lesson: Don't throw away those old vinyl records.

JAN BEUCKELZOON

Revolutionary

WORST DEEDS: Using a 1533 guest sermon on Anabaptism in Münster, Germany, to incite its citizens to immediately overthrow all the city's civil and church authorities ★ Running through the streets naked for three days then declaring himself King Jan, ruler of New Zion and the entire world ★ Burning artworks and all books except the Bible while seizing private property and declaring a communal state, where all goods and land would be jointly owned after he had skimmed off the best of it for himself ★ Commanding all single women to submit to polygamous marriages, then taking 15 wives for himself ★ Enforcing a new strict legal code with death sentences carried out on anyone, including children, who committed even minor sins such as lying and arguing ★ Beheading one of his wives for being rude to him, then forcing the others to dance around her corpse in celebration ★ Bringing on a famine that forced his subjects to devour rats, insects, grass, leather, and each other, while he continued to eat well ★ Being finally captured, then tortured for six months before being executed and having his body hung in a cage from a church tower in Münster, where his body was left to rot for 50 years (the cages are still there) ★ Appalling Martin Luther, leader of the country's original Baptist movement, so thoroughly that Luther put aside his pacifist beliefs and called for the violent overthrow and execution of Jan Beuckelzoon and all his followers

BORN: 1509 in Leiden, Germany

DIED: 1536

NICKNAME: "John of Leiden"

FIRST JOB: Tailor

HOW TO STAY FIT IN PRISON

MENTALLY FIT

⭐ Accept your circumstances.

Realize right away that prison will prevent you from meeting many of your fundamental psychological needs, such as privacy and freedom. Adjust to it instead of becoming increasingly frustrated, angry, and deluded.

⭐ Make friends with the guards.

Demonstrate your admirable qualities and obey their instructions. Avoid the temptation to lash back if they goad you. Build the relationship slowly over time. Guards can become valuable in gaining information about the outside world and in providing you with someone to talk to.

⭐ Exercise your brain.

Read as much educational material as possible. Focus on gaining new knowledge and expertise. If you are denied access to reading materials, regularly engage in mental exercises. Recite the basic multiplication tables, then extend them higher and higher. Do long division in your head. Compose letters and poetry. Review lists of facts and figures you memorized early in life. Think of important issues and argue both sides. Use a deck of cards to play memory games.

Exercise at the same time every day or twice a day.

★ | Play music.
Whistle, sing, drum, or engage in another musical activity. Compose and perform songs using whatever instruments you can improvise, like drumming on the bars.

★ | Meditate.
Use the long periods of inactivity and lulls of prison to meditate. Close your eyes. Breathe deeply and regularly. Empty your mind and try to think of nothing at all, or concentrate on a single image or idea. Make this a daily part of your routine.

★ | Plot your future.
Think of what you are going to do when you leave prison. List your post-prison goals and all the things you will need to do to fulfill them. Add more details each time you think about it.

PHYSICALLY FIT

★ | Develop a routine.
Exercise at the same time every day or twice a day. An hour before mealtime is ideal so your muscles will be refueled by food.

★ | Do cardiovascular activities.
Use the prison track or any other cardio exercise facilities. If you are confined in a small cell, run in place, do jumping jacks, or dance vigorously. Use cardio to warm up your muscles for strength exercises and on its own to strengthen your heart and legs.

★ **Do bunk pull-ups.**
Get a firm grip on the end of the metal bed frame on the top bunk in your cell. Lift your legs so you are suspended in the air, then pull your chin up over the bar using the muscles in your shoulders, arms, and upper back.

★ **Do bar back pulls.**
Grab one of the bars of your cell, one hand on top of the other while standing an arm's length away. Use your upper back muscles to slowly pull yourself toward the bars. Relax and return to your original position and repeat. Reverse the position of your hands and perform a second set.

★ **Do cellmate squats.**
Ask your cellmate to sit on your shoulders while you perform leg squats. Do not allow your upper legs to dip past parallel to the ground to avoid putting too much stress on your legs. If you are in solitary confinement, place any available heavy object on your shoulders or just do more repetitions of straight squats.

★ **Do hanging sit-ups.**
Lay on your bed with the upper half of your body hanging over the edge of your mattress. Perform a set of sit-ups, emphasizing the lower part of your abdomen. Then lay flat on your back on the bed and curl your knees slowly to your chest using the upper part of your ab muscles.

★ Do floor and wall push-ups.
Perform a set of push-ups on the floor, focusing on using your pectoral, shoulder, and arm muscles. Then stand and lean at a 45-degree angle against a wall and perform another set of push-ups. The angled push-ups will develop the upper part of your pectoral muscles.

★ Do towel pulls.
Hold a rolled-up shower towel, sheet, or blanket in front of your chest and pull your arms apart in opposite directions using your pectoral and shoulder muscles.

Political Brief

In 1974, Ugandan dictator Idi Amin put 138 French tourists under armed guard in a Ugandan hotel to convince French film-maker Barbet Schroeder to cut two and a half minutes of "unflattering" footage from his documentary *Idi Amin Dada*. Amin, a former army officer who executed an estimated 300,000 people during his reign from 1971–79, took the hostages after he found out Paris audiences were laughing at him during the screening of the film. After Amin forced dozens of the hostages to call the filmmaker at his home in France to plead with him, Schroeder re-edited the movie to fit Amin's specifications.

EMPEROR'S RUN OF GOOD LUCK TURNS TO LIFE OF UNRELENTING MISERY

As a newborn in 1740, Ivan Antonovich was declared heir apparent to the throne of Russia by his grand aunt and acting empress Anna Ivanovna. When Anna died of kidney disease two months later, he became Ivan VI, Emperor of Russia. But just over a year after his ascension, Ivan was overthrown by Elizabeth, daughter of Peter the Great. Though he lived another 22 years, Ivan VI would never spend another hour as emperor or as a free man. Fearing that her enemies might try to replace her on the throne with Ivan, Elizabeth imprisoned Ivan with his family in Siberia, then in solitary confinement on an island fortress on the Newa River. Ivan was placed in a dark room without windows and forbidden to speak even to his guards, who did not know his identity. In 1762, Elizabeth died and was succeeded by Peter III. The new monarch visited Ivan in prison with an eye to naming him as his successor. Ivan, by then insane, told Peter that he was not actually Ivan, but a surrogate occupying the body of Ivan, who had ascended to heaven years ago. Peter changed his mind about naming Ivan successor and ordered him put in chains and tortured. Peter was assassinated after just six months on the throne by his wife, Catherine the Great, leading to yet another decline in Ivan's fortunes. Vasily Yakovlevich Mirovich, a second lieutenant at Ivan's island fortress, guessed Ivan's identity. Hostile to Catherine's rule, Mirovich organized a rescue of Ivan so he could be restored to the throne. As Mirovich and his fellow conspirators approached Ivan's cell, his guards murdered Ivan on the orders of Catherine, who insisted Ivan should never be freed. The 23-year-old ex-emperor was buried in an unmarked grave.

Political Lesson: Don't assume good fortune early in your career will last.

Political Comebacks

Who	Previous Position	Down and Out	Comeback
Earl Long	Governor of Louisiana	Confined in an insane asylum	Won Democratic nomination to represent Louisiana in the U.S. House of Representatives after he was released from the asylum
Richard Nixon	Vice President of the United States (1953–61)	Lost 1960 presidential election, then lost the 1962 race for governor of California	Won 1968 election to become president of the United States
Nelson Mandela	Leading anti-apartheid activist in South Africa during the 1950s and '60s	Spent 27 years in prison on conspiracy and sabotage charges	Helped bring an end to apartheid and won election to become South Africa's president (1994–99)
Adolf Hitler	Head of Germany's Nazi Party (1921–24)	Failed to take over the country with a pathetic coup attempt; served six months in prison	Rebuilt the Nazi Party after his release and became Chancellor of Germany ten years later, then dictator
Marion Barry	Mayor of Washington, D.C. (1979–91)	Caught on video smoking crack in hotel room with former mistress, forced to resign as mayor and serve six months in federal prison	Was elected mayor again in 1994
Alan García Pérez	President of Peru (1985–90)	Forced to leave office and flee the country as Peru sank into civil war, over 50 percent unemployment, and a 7000 percent annual inflation rate	Reclaimed presidency in 2006

SELECTED SOURCES

Articles

Cantor, Doug. "Five of the largest, oddest and most useless state projects," CNN.com, 27 July 2007.

Cathcarth, Michael. "Lemonade Ley: Minister for Murder." *Australian Broadcasting Corporation*, 7 November 2004.

Fitch, Robert. "How Ross Perot Made a Quarter Billion Dollars Running for President." *The Perot Periodical*, Fall 1993.

French, Howard. "Anatomy of an Autocracy: Mobutu's 32-Year Reign." *The New York Times*, 17 May 1997.

_____."In One Swift Hour." *Time*, 28 July 1958.

Joyce, Kolin. "Sacked Governor to Challenge Japan's Old Guard." *Daily Telegraph*, 15 July 2002.

Kautz, Pete. "The Original Cassius Clay." *Close Quarters Combat Magazine*, 2002.

King, Laura. "Angry Mob Kills Afghan Minister." Associated Press, 15 February 2002.

Koerner, Brendan I. "How Did Suharto Steal $35 Billion?" Slate.com, 26 March 2004.

Link, Perry. "Will SARS Transform China's Chiefs?" *Time*, 28 April 2003.

_____."The Man Who Was King." *Time*, 25 August 1958.

Miller, Tom. "Tricky Dick." *The New Yorker*, 30 August 2004.

Moody, John. "Bad Times for Baby Doc." *Time*, 24 June 2001.

Moran, Tom. "A State of Corruption." *The Star Ledger*, 10 November 2002.

Palumbo, Gene. "Suspicion Lingers in Salvadorian Bishop's Murder." *National Catholic Reporter*, 16 July 1993.

_____. "Paul Ended Our Marriage at a Dinner Party." *Sydney Morning Herald*, 20 April 2004.

Roberts, Sam. "Sex, Politics and Murder on the Potomac." *The New York Times*, 1 March 1992.

Smolowe, Jill. "The Philippines." *Time*, 9 February 1987.

Stavrou, Phillip. "Political Sex Scandals: Ancient History in Ottawa." CTV News, 5 May 2007.

Taibbi, Matt. "Boris Yeltsin: Death of a Drunk." *Rolling Stone*, 11 August 2006.

Tempest, Matthew. "Profile: Sir Mark Thatcher." *Guardian Unlimited*, 25 August 2004.

Turner, Corey. "Idi Amin Film Prompts Viewing of 1974 Documentary." National Public Radio, 2 November 2006.

Books

Barrett, Anthony. *Agrippina: Sex, Power and Politics in the Early Roman Empire*. Yale University Press, 1996.

Bernstein, Carl, and Bob Woodward. *All the President's Men*. Simon & Schuster, 1974.

Bevan, E.R. *The House of Ptolemy*. Methuen Publishing, 1927.

Beyer, Rick. *The Greatest Stories Never Told*. HarperCollins, 2003.

Boardman, John (editor), Jasper Griffin (editor), and Oswyn Murray (editor). *The Oxford Illustrated History of Greece and the Hellenistic World*. Oxford University Press, 2001.

Bogard, Cynthia J. *Seasons Such as These: How Homelessness Took Shape in America*. Aldine de Gruyter, 2003.

Brandt, Nat. *The Congressman Who Got Away with Murder*. Syracuse University Press, 1992.

Caro, Robert A. *The Path to Power: The Years of Lyndon Johnson (Vol. I)*. Knopf, 1982.

Carpini, John de Plano. *The Long and Wonderful Voyage of Friar John de Plano Carpini*. Originally published in 1246.

Churchill, Ward. *Struggle for the Land*. City Lights Books, 2002.

Clark, Sir Kenneth. *Civilization*. John Murray, 1980.

Dangerfield, George. *The Era of Good Feelings: America Comes of Age in the Period of Monroe and Adams*. Harbinger, 1963.

Dunham, Mikel. *Buddha's Warriors: The Story of the CIA-Backed Tibetan Freedom Fighters, the Chinese Communist Invasion and the Ultimate Fall of Tibet*. Tarcher, 2004.

Elson, Henry. *History of the United States of America*. Macmillan, 1904.

Foss, Clive. *The Tyrants: 2500 Years of Absolute Power and Corruption*. Quercus Publishing, 2006.

French, Howard. *A Continent for the Taking: The Tragedy and Hope of Africa*. Vintage, 2005.

Gay, Peter. *The Age of Enlightenment.* Time-Life Books, 1966.

Gibbon, Edward. *The Decline and Fall of the Roman Empire.* Modern Library, 2003.

Gilbert, William. *Renaissance and Reformation.* Carrie, 1998.

Godoy, Don Manuel de. *Memoirs.* R. Bentley, 1836.

Goodrich, Samuel Griswold. *A History of All Nations.* Miller, Orton, and Mulligan, 1856.

Green, Peter. *Alexander to Actium: The Historical Evolution of the Hellenistic Age.* University of California Press, 1993.

James, Marquis. *The Raven: A Biography of Sam Houston.* Bobbs Merrill, 1929.

Keay, John. *India: A History.* Grove Press, 2001.

Keneally, Thomas. *American Scoundrel: The Life of the Notorious Civil War General Dan Sickles.* Anchor, 2003.

Livy, Titus. *The Early History of Rome.* Penguin Classics, 2002.

Marcus, Greil. *Lipstick Traces: A Secret History of the 20th Century.* Harvard University Press, 1990.

Mastrini, Hana. *Frommer's Prague and the Best of the Czech Republic (Sixth Edition).* Frommer's, 2006

McCullough, David. *John Adams.* Simon & Schuster, 2001.

Paine, Albert Bigelow. *Thomas Nast: His Period and His Pictures.* Pyne Press, 1974.

Plutarch. *Lives (Vols. 1 & II).* Modern Library, 2001.

Reader, John. *Africa: A Biography of the Continent.* Vintage, 1999.

Schmidt, Karl J. *An Atlas and Survey of South Asian History.* M.E. Sharpe, 1997.

Seutonius, Tranquillus. *The Lives of the Twelve Caesars.* Echo Library, 2006.

Shirer, William L. *The Rise and Fall of the Third Reich: A History of Nazi Germany.* Simon & Schuster, 1960.

Southern, R.W. *Western Society and the Church in the Middle Ages.* Penguin, 1990.

Tacitus. *The Complete Works of Tacitus.* McGraw-Hill, 1964.

Tuchman, Barbara. *A Distant Mirror: The Calamitous 14th Century.* Balantine Books, 1987.

Wallace, Amy, and David Wallechinsky. *The New Book of Lists: The Original Compendium of Curious Information.* Canaongate, 2005.

Walthall, Anne. *Peasant Uprisings in Japan*. University of Chicago Press, 1991.

Web sites

Air Force Wives (www.airforcewives.com)

All Africa (www.allafrica.com)

Amazing Australia (www.amazingaustralia.com)

Australian Politics (Australianpolitics.com)

Bartlett's Quotations (www.bartleby.com/100)

Biographical Directory of the United States Congress (Bioguide.congress.gov/biosearch/biosearch.asp)

British Broadcasting Corporation History Site (BBC.co.uk/history)

Canadian Encyclopedia (Canadianencyclopedia.com)

Columbia World of Quotations (www.bartleby.com/66)

Decameron Web (www.brown.edu/Departments/Italian_Studies/dweb/dweb.shtml)

Encyclopedia Britannica Online (www.britannica.com)

Encyclopedia of World History (www.bartleby.com/67)

History Buff (Historybuff.com)

I, Claudius Project (www.anselm.edu/internet/classics/I%2CCLAUDIUS/information.html)

Internet History Sourcebooks Project (www.fordham.edu/halsall)

Irish History Gateway (www.academicinfo.net/histirish.htm)

Library of Congress Country Studies (lcweb2.loc.gov/frd/cs/cshome.html)

Livius Articles on Ancient History (www.brown.edu/Departments/Italian_Studies/dweb/dweb.shtml)

Military History (www.militaryhistoryonline.com)

National Geographic (www.nationalgeographic.com)

Palaces (www.historicroyalpalaces.org)

Paul Keating Insults Archive (www.webcity.com.au/keating)

Pennsylvania Historical and Museum Commission (www.phmc.state.pa.us)

Political Graveyard (www.politicalgraveyard.com)

PBS American Experience (www.pbs.org/wgbh/amex)

PBS Frontline (www.pbs.org/wgbh/pages/frontline)

Questia (www.questia.com)

The Skeleton Closet (www.realchange.org)

Slate (www.slate.com)

Southern Baptist University (users.sbuniv.edu/~hgallatin/hil3le25.html)

Spartacus Educational (www.spartacus.schoolnet.co.uk)

United States Central Intelligence Agency World Factbook
   (www.cia.gov/library/publications/the-world-factbook/geos/fo.html)

Urban Legends – Dan Quayle Quotes (www.snopes.com/quotes/quayle.a)

Victorian Web (www.victorianweb.org)

VoltaireNet (www.voltairenet.org)

Wikipedia (www.wikipedia.org)

Women's History (www.womenshistory.about.com)

Newspapers, Magazines, Other Media

Billings Gazette

The Boston Globe

Chicago Tribune

The Christian Science Monitor

Daily Times of Nigeria

Discovery Channel

Encyclopedia Americana

Encyclopedia Britannica

The Guardian

Hindustan Times

The History Channel

Indo-Asian News Service

International Herald Tribune

Jane's Defence Weekly

Los Angeles Times

Melbourne's *Herald Sun*

National Catholic Reporter

National Review

The New York Times

The New Yorker

Newsweek

Rolling Stone

Smithsonian

Der Spiegel

The Sydney Morning Herald

The Toronto Star

U.S. News & World Report

U.S. State Department

The Washington Post

INDEX

Ferdinand VII (king of Spain), 187, 190
Ferris, Jeannie, 90–91
Fiji Coup, 50–51
filibusters and other delaying tactics, 97–99
Fillmore, Millard, 135
First Serbian Uprising, 234
Fischer, Joschka, 14
fitness in prison, 237–41
Foley, Mark, 140–41
Foot, Michael, 134
foreign faux pas, 175
fortunes amassed in office, 167
Foxe, Fanne, 151
France, faux pas in, 175
Frederick I (Holy Roman Emperor), 217
French Revolution, 234

G Galba, 81
Gandy, Fred, 204
García Pérez, Alan, 243
Garfield, James, 216
Garrett, Peter, 123
Gegeo, Kamal Hana, 27
George IV (king of England), 134
George V (king of England), 175
Ghana, faux pas in, 175
Gibbons, Jim, 116
Gibraltar, 209
Gillars, Mildred, 187
Glickman, Dan, 61
Goldstein, Hymann, 138
Goldwater, Barry, 73, 128
Gorbachev, Mikhail, 222

Gowon, Yakubu, 123
Great Jewish Revolt, 234
Great She Elephant Ntombazi (queen of Ndwande Tribe), 217
Greece, faux pas in, 175
Greendor, Keith, 138
Gregory VII (pope), 200
Grey, Jane, 40
Gulf War, first, 206
Guyuk (Great Khan of Mongolia), 201

H Halpin, Maria, 149
Hamlin, Hannibal, 48
Harcourt, Michael, 142
Hart, Gary, 105
Henry II (king of England), 198–99
Henry III (king of England), 49
Henry IV (Holy Roman Emperor), 200
Henry VI (king of England), 63
Henry VII (king of England), 34
Hesketh, Graham "The Baron," 27
Hess, Rudolph, 195
Higashikokubaru, Hideo, 35, 203
Hills, Carla, 189
Hinson, Jon C., 150
Hitler, Adolf, 194, 229, 243
Hockey, Joe, 83
Holland, John, 202
hostile room, working, 87–89
Houston, Eliza, 29
Houston, Sam, 29
Howard, John, 83, 123
Hsieh, Frank, 79

ACKNOWLEDGMENTS

Turk Regan would like to thank Sarah O'Brien for being a great editor, George W. Bush for ushering in a golden age for political humorists, and Dr. Jim Soles for being the best-case scenario political science professor and an all-around fine human being.

David Borgenicht would, of course, like to thank his beautiful wife and wonderful children, without whose support and understanding his campaign would not have been possible. He would also like to thank his amazing campaign managers and spin-meisters, Sarah O'Brien, Jay Schaefer, Steve Mockus, Brianna Smith, Doug Ogan, Beth Steiner, and Aya Akazawa—as well as Karen Onorato, his campaign designer, and Brenda Brown, his campaign illustrator. All of you have places in his cabinet. Not on staff, of course—but he's got a really big cabinet that you'll all fit inside. Finally, he'd like to thank all of the little people who gave their time and energy to his campaign, as well as his corporate sponsors, Halliburton, McDonnell Douglas, and Chi-Chi's. Without them, none of this would have been possible. And as usual, just make those checks out to his given name, "Cash."

ABOUT THE AUTHORS

David Borgenicht is the creator and coauthor of all the books in the *Worst-Case Scenario* series, and is president and publisher of Quirk Books (www.quirkbooks.com). Since his year-long stint as Senior Class Vice President in high school, he has never run for elected office, instead devoting his attention (like Jimmy Carter and Bill Clinton) to books, international relations, and charity work. He lives in Philadelphia.

Turk Regan turned to writing after his career in politics was cut short by a tragic handshaking accident. He has authored numerous articles and books, including Pimp My Cubicle, the Hillary Clinton Voodoo Kit, and the George W. Bush Voodoo Kit. He splits his time between living in the state of California and a state of disbelief.

Brenda Brown is an illustrator and cartoonist whose work has been published in many books and publications, including the *Worst-Case Scenario* series, *Esquire*, *Reader's Digest*, *USA Weekend*, *21st Century Science & Technology*, the *Saturday Evening Post*, and the *National Enquirer*. Her Web site is www.webtoon.com.

THE FIRST OF THE WORST

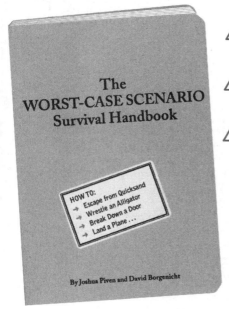

⚠ 3 million copies in print

⚠ Translated into 27 languages

⚠ International best-seller

"An armchair guide for the anxious."
—*USA Today*

"The book to have when the killer bees arrive."
—*The New Yorker*

"Nearly 180 pages of immediate action drills for when everything goes to hell in a handbasket."
—*Soldier of Fortune*

"This is a really nifty book."
—*Forbes*

A BOOK FOR EVERY DISASTER

MORE WORST-CASE SCENARIOS FOR EVERY SEASON

→ The Worst-Case Scenario Daily Survival Calendar
→ The Worst-Case Scenario Daily Survival Calendar: Golf
→ The Worst-Case Scenario Dating & Sex Address Book
→ The Worst-Case Scenario Sticky Situation Notes

Watch for these WORST-CASE SCENARIO games at retailers near you or at:

VISIT

www.chroniclebooks.com/worstcase
to order books and read excerpts

www.worstcasescenarios.com
for updates, new scenarios, and more!

Because you just never know…

3 1901 04875 7266